High Sierra
Hiking Guide

Devils Postpile

including the Ritter Range,
the Mammoth Lakes area,
and parts of the John Muir
and Ansel Adams Wildernesses

Ron Felzer

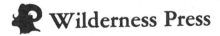 **Wilderness Press**

BERKELEY

First edition 1971
Second edition 1976
Third edition 1982
Fourth edition 1986
FIFTH EDITION 1990

Copyright © 1971, 1976, 1982, 1986, 1990 by Ron Felzer
Photos by the author except as noted
Design by Thomas Winnett
Library of Congress Card Number 89-70727
International Standard Book Number 0-89997-111-3
Manufactured in the United States

Published by   Wilderness Press
                2440 Bancroft Way
                Berkeley, CA 94704
                (415) 843-8080
                Write for free catalog

Library of Congress Cataloging-in-Publication Data

Felzer, Ron.
    Devils Postpile: including the Ritter Range and Mammoth Lakes
area / Ron Felzer. -- 5th ed.
        p. cm. --(High Sierra hiking guide)
    Includes bibliographical references
    ISBN 0-89997-111-3
    1. Hiking--California--Devils Postpile National Monument--Guide
-books. 2. Devils Postpile National Monument (Calif.)--Guide-books.
I. Title. II. Series: High Sierra hiking guide (1986)
GV199.42.C22D483 1990
917.94'4--dc20   89-70727
                                                           CIP

Location of the area covered by this guide

Introduction

The HIGH SIERRA HIKING GUIDES are the first *complete* guides to the famous High Sierra. Each guide covers *at least* one entire 15-minute U.S.G.S. topographic quadrangle, which is an area about 14 miles east-west by 17 miles north-south. The inside front cover shows the location of the area covered by this guide.

There is a great and increasing demand for literature about America's favorite wilderness, John Muir's "Range of Light." To meet this demand, Wilderness Press has undertaken this guide series. The purpose of each book in the series is threefold: first, to provide a reliable basis for planning a trip; second, to serve as a field guide while you are on the trail; and third, to stimulate you to further field investigation and background reading. In each guide, there are a minimum of 100 described miles of trails, and the descriptions are supplemented with maps and other logistical and background information. HIGH SIERRA HIKING GUIDES are based on firsthand observation. There is absolutely no substitute for walking the trails, so we walked all the trails.

In planning this series, we chose the 15-minute quadrangle as the unit because—though every way of dividing the Sierra is arbitrary—the quadrangle map is the chosen aid of almost every wilderness traveler. Inside the back cover of this book is a Wilderness Press map of the quadrangle showing the described trails. With this map, you can always get where you want to go, with a minimum of detours or wasted effort. (There is also a Wilderness Press edition of the *Merced Peak* quadrangle, showing the western end of Backpack Trails #3 and #11.)

There is one other thing you will need: a **wilderness permit** from the Forest Service (for federally designated wilderness areas) or from the National Park Service (for national-park backcountry). You may obtain a permit at a Park Service or Forest Service ranger station or office by indicating where you are going and when you will be there. Forest Service permit reservations are available by mail. For westside entry into the Ansel Adams Wilderness, write Sierra National Forest, North Fork, CA 93643. For eastside entry into the Ansel Adams Wilderness, write Inyo National Forest, Box 148, Mammoth Lakes, CA 93546 or Inyo National Forest, Box 429, Lee Vining, CA 93541. For eastside entry into John Muir Wilderness, write Inyo National Forest, 873 N. Main St., Bishop, CA 93514. Advance trail reservations can be made by mail between March 1 and May 31 for travel between July 1 and September 15, and there is a newly instituted $3 per person advance reservation fee for this service. Permits may be obtained in person at the Mammoth Ranger Station in Mammoth Lakes and at Devils Postpile National Monument the first day of a hike. During the peak summer season (July and August), however, trail quotas are often filled early in the day, so it is best to inquire about summer permits *several months* in advance, especially for large groups.

When you get your permit, you might be warned that during the past decade black-bear raids on improperly stored food have become an increasing problem in the Devils Postpile area, particularly at Agnew Meadows. Federal law and common sense both require that all food be stored safely when not attended.

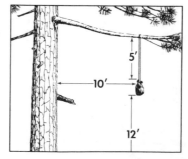

Recommended *minimum* distances for bearbagging on a tree branch.

Contents

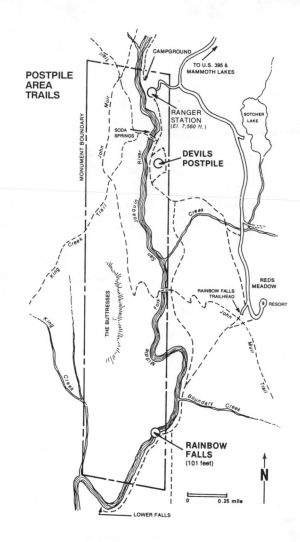

POSTPILE
AREA
TRAILS

CAMPGROUND

TO U.S. 395 &
MAMMOTH LAKES

RANGER
STATION
(El. 7,560 ft.)

SOTCHER
LAKE

SODA
SPRINGS

DEVILS
POSTPILE

MONUMENT BOUNDARY

John   Muir   Trail

San   Joaquin   River

Creek

King   Creek

THE BUTTRESSES

Middle   Fork

RAINBOW FALLS
TRAILHEAD

REDS
MEADOW

RESORT

John   Muir   Trail

King   Creek

Boundary   Creek

RAINBOW
FALLS
(101 feet)

LOWER FALLS

0   0.25 mile

N

The Country

GAZING WEST FROM Minaret Summit, near the eastern edge of the quadrangle, the first-time visitor to Mammoth Lakes and the Devils Postpile country is stunned with awe at the grand vista below.

The jagged, knife-edged Minarets, products of volcanic activity around 150 million years ago, dominate the skyline. Mt. Ritter and Banner Peak, the highest points in the quadrangle (at 13,157 and 12,945 feet, respectively) stand to their right. This is great country to climb in.

Fifteen hundred feet below the viewer is the glacially scraped and rounded canyon of the Middle Fork of the San Joaquin River, which originates north of Banner Peak at Thousand Island Lake and flows across the quadrangle from north to south. Way off in the southwest, the impassable canyons of the lower Middle Fork and the lower North Fork merge on their way to slake the thirst of the Central Valley. There's plenty of water here.

More than a dozen major year-round streams drain the backcountry. Over 50 trout lakes in glaciated basins dot the mountainsides. Glaciers, permanent snowfields and deep winter snowpacks keep them flowing and cold. This is great country for fishing.

Inyo National Forest and Devils Postpile National Monument maintain a dozen automobile campgrounds in the quadrangle. There are more than 150 miles of backcountry trails with innumerable campsites. Hiking and backpacking possibilities abound.

Behind the viewer is Mammoth Mountain, an ancient volcano. Red cinder cones are just out of sight to the south. To the north and east are explosion craters and an earthquake fissure. Then there is Devils Postpile itself, down near the Middle Fork of the San Joaquin. In this quadrangle the geologist has a field day.

A variety of plant communities—from yellow-pine forest to alpine fell-fields to sagebrush scrub—beckon the botanist.

The first-time viewer perusing this vast and varied environment sees many possibilities here. Whether car-camper, sightseer, photographer, angler, naturalist, hiker or mountain climber, he may become one of the many who return again and again. Though the land visible from Minaret Summit may lose some of its novelty, it will remain "not a place to make time, but to spend it."

The Ritter Range from Minaret Summit

The History

INDIANS DISCOVERED the Sierra long before mountain man Jedediah Smith in 1827 led the first crossing of the range by Europeans. Several parties under Joseph Walker went through Owens Valley and passed by Mono Lake between 1834 and 1846, but for several years after, whites had little impact on either the Yokut Indians to the west of *Devils Postpile* quadrangle or the Paiutes in the Great Basin country to the east.

Yokuts and Paiutes had been trading over Mono pass for hundreds of years before a cavalry detachment—in pursuit of Yosemite Indian Chief Teneiya—first crossed the Sierra in this region in 1852, going down Bloody Canyon, which lies just north of our quad. These soldiers soon returned to the west side, bringing back little more than some observations on gold-bearing quartz veins and obsidian domes east of the Sierra.

The demise of the native American way of life in this part of the Sierra was begun by the Gold Rush in the Mother Lode to the west and by mining activities in the Comstock Lode to the north. In the Mammoth Lakes region, this destruction of a gentle people came in the late 1870s. The killing of game and the destruction of natural forage by cattle were among the processes that forever disrupted the lives of the native inhabitants east of the crest. Most of the Paiutes who weren't killed off by white ranchers and miners went to work for them.

Probably the most significant early event in the development of human influence in this quadrangle was the incorporation of the Mammoth Mining Company in 1878. "Bonanzas" that didn't work out nevertheless led to a flurry of mining activity in the Mammoth Lakes area from 1877 to 1880. In 1878 the 54-mile Mammoth Trail, from Fresno Flats to Mammoth City via Reds Meadow and Mammoth Pass, became for stockmen, ranchers and prospectors a direct route

across the Sierra to Mammoth Lakes. The droughts of 1863-
64, '71 and '77 drove stockmen to the mountains for summer
grazing. Sheepherding continued as far east as Summit
Meadow until 1963. Mining at Mammoth City was pretty
much a bust by 1880, but prospecting and spasms of activity
in the late 1890s and again in the 1920s continued to open
up the country.

In 1907 President Theodore Roosevelt proclaimed the
formation of Inyo National Forest, consisting mostly of acreage
in Owens Valley. Today half of our quadrangle lies in Inyo
National Forest and half in Sierra National Forest. This land is
administered by the government largely for recreation and
watershed purposes. Devils Postpile National Monument,
established in 1911, is the only other large ownership in the
quad. So the main economic activities in this area have
progressed from spates of mining and grazing to recreation,
with some timber harvesting as well.

The John Muir and Minarets wildernesses were
established in 1964 to protect much pristine country in *Devils
Postpile* quadrangle. The Wilderness Act of 1984 greatly
expanded the Minarets Wilderness, extending protection to
the previously threatened San Joaquin corridor, and renaming
the whole area the Ansel Adams Wilderness. These changes
have not come about painlessly, and such issues as rampant
overdevelopment in Mammoth Lakes and expansion of the
Mammoth Mountain and June Mountain ski areas are being
hotly debated now.

The Geology

LANDFORMS RESULTING from volcanism and glaciation dominate the landscape of *Devils Postpile* quadrangle. Pumice flats, red cinder cones and ancient lava flows attest to the past unheavals of this land. U-shaped canyons, hanging valleys, and scraped and polished rock faces show the grinding force of the most recent Ice Age glaciers on the underlying granitic and metamorphoric rocks of the quadrangle

Expanses of a porous, lightweight volcanic rock called pumice cover much of the eastern portion of the quadrangle. Pumice is a grayish, glassy rock full of holes created by gas expanding within the erupting, molten lava. Eruptions have occurred from about 40,000 years ago to about 1400 A.D., from vents that lie on a line from Mammoth Mountain to Mono Lake. These vents were formed when superheated gases and lava blew into the air at weak spots in the earth's crust.

Devils Postpile, from which this quadrangle takes its name, is itself a product of volcanism. A little less than 100,000 years ago dark, molten lava of a type called basalt poured through Mammoth Pass and flowed down the canyon of the Middle Fork of the San Joaquin River. Here the liquid rock cooled, solidified, contracted and cracked to form columns having from three to seven sides. Later, glaciers scraped the tops of these vertical columns and left a beautiful, tilelike surface of glacial polish that can still be seen today.

As much as any other geologic process, glaciation has determined what the traveler in *Devils Postpile* quadrangle experiences. During the last approximately three million years, the Sierra probably experienced many glaciations. These were times when winter snowfall greatly exceeded summer snowmelt, ice fields formed, and rivers of ice began to flow down from the high country. These glaciers carved out glacial basins, called cirques, surrounded on three sides by narrow ridges, called arêtes, which the ice never overtopped.

Glaciers in large canyons, like that of the Middle Fork of the San Joaquin, cut deeper than the tributary glaciers, leaving the tributary valleys "hanging," with cascades coming down from them—such as Shadow Creek.

As these rivers of ice advanced, they scraped, gouged and plucked vast amounts of material from the underlying rock, and pushed and carried this material to lower elevations. When the glaciers melted back, they left ridges of piled rock called moraines along the sides of canyons and across them.

Glacial polish, which is especially evident along the Shadow Creek Trail and between Reds Meadow and Fish Valley, evinces the grinding force of the ice with its load of rock debris. Further testimony to the glaciers' power are the *roches moutonees* seen along the North and Middle forks of the San Joaquin. A *roche moutonee* is a large hump of rock with a steep downstream face, where the glacier plucked material away, and a gently sloping upstream side, planed by the advancing ice.

This recent glacial erosion is one important reason that most canyon walls are so devoid of vegetation compared to canyon floors. The ice scoured the canyon walls and deposited the material on the canyon floors, where it developed into soil hospitable to plant growth.

Geological events, modified by the effects of climate, determine not only what rocks we walk on during the day, but also to a large degree what plant cover we sleep under at night, and even whether there's wood for a campfire.

The Flora

THIS CHAPTER EMPHASIZES that part of the flora we call trees. Not only are trees the most evident members of the plant kingdom in *Devils Postpile* quadrangle, but they exert the greatest influence on environmental conditions that determine what other plants and what animals are to be found. Trees affect the incoming solar energy and the outgoing reflected and reradiated energy, and hence affect the temperature. They modify atmospheric humidity. They modify the wind; they change the very earth itself by their root actions, and by their litter of dead leaves, limbs and trunks which eventually return to the soil.

Lodgepole pine (*Pinus murrayana*) is far and away the most abundant tree in the quadrangle. It is found from about 7000 to 10,000 feet in elevation, and from canyon bottoms to windwept summits. Lodgepole is easily distinguished from all other conifers in the region by its 2-inch-long needles grouped in bundles of two; its thin, scaly, light-colored bark; and its short, prickly cones, which may remain closed and on the tree for several years. This latter feature ties right in with the ecology of the species.

Lodgepole belongs to an amorphous group of plants called "pioneer" species because they are among the first to enter and establish themselves in an area that has been disturbed. Sometimes lodgepole cones remain closed until the heat of a forest fire opens them to release the seeds. The winged seeds are easily carried by the wind onto burned areas, landslides, avalanche slopes and road cuts, where they quickly germinate and cover the ground with a dense growth of seedlings.

This pioneering character of lodgepole pine is tied in with the species' intolerance of shade. Seedlings do very poorly under the cover of larger trees even parent lodgepoles—and regeneration is much better in openings than under the forest canopy. That is one reason why, in meadows throughout our quadrangle, lodgepole-pine forest is succeeding grasses. If seedlings can get started in the generally heavy turf of meadows, they grow fast, because of favorable light and moisture conditions. Fires, which kill both small and large lodgepoles, and sheep, which kill just about everything, have tended in the past to keep High Sierra meadows in what ecologists call a "subclimax" condition, consisting of grasses and herbs. These nonwoody plants withstand the onslaught of grazers better than trees do because of their shorter life cycles. However, Smoky the Bear and restrictions on grazing in the mountains have led to the invasion of many meadows— Summit Meadow in particular—by lodgepole pine. Eventually the shade-tolerant but fire-intolerant firs may succeed even lodgepole pines in this ecological process. Firs replacing themselves would be the "climax" community here, until fire or some other disturbance set the forest back to an earlier stage.

Another pine, found generally at somewhat lower elevations and on drier sites than lodgepole, is Jeffrey pine (*Pinus jeffreyi*). It was named for its discoverer, John Jeffrey, an early Scots botanist who, when the Royal Society was slow in sending him his stipend, walked off into the Mojave Desert never to be heard from again. Jeffrey pine is similar to ponderosa, or yellow pine, a species found mostly lower down on the west slope of the Sierra and not at all in *Devils Postpile* quad east of the Sierra crest. Jeffrey is distinguished by its large, stiff cones (5-12″) and the heavily vanilla- or root-beer-scented bark of older specimens. Its 5-10″ needles are nearly always in groups of three, and they often appear from a distance to be clumped at branch ends. Jeffrey may be distinguished from lodgepole pine not only by its needles but also by its bark, which is dark and furrowed on young trees and reddish in large plates on older ones.

The ecology of Jeffreys contrasts with that of lodgepoles in that Jeffreys are more fire-resistant, due to thicker bark, and tend to form uneven-aged stands of trees of varying ages, compared to the more homogeneously aged groves of lodgepole.

Its roots were used by early California natives in basketwork.

Jeffrey pine ranges from Oregon to Baja California, and in *Devils Postpile* quadrangle it is normally found between 6000 and 9000 feet. It is common on the trail to Cascade Valley.

Western white pine (*Pinus monticola*) is one of several 5-needle pines encountered in our quad. Another one commonly encountered here is whitebark pine. "Five-needle pines" are those whose needles are grouped in bundles ("fascicles") of five. Within the group are also sugar pine, limber pine, bristlecone pine and eastern white pine. Western white pine's flexible-scaled cones are 5-10" long, and its bark is brownish and blocky. Once the mainstay of the timber industry in Idaho, this species has just about been wiped out commercially in the northern part of its range by white-pine blister rust. This disease, which attacks all 5-needle pines, was brought into this country in the late 19th century on seedlings from Europe. Like many introduced parasites, blister rust had no natural enemies in the new habitat, and its new hosts had no immunity to it, so it spread fast and destructively. An interesting feature of this fungus' life cycle is that it lives on 5-needle pines for part of its life and on members of the genus *Ribes*—gooseberries and currants—for the other part. Both groups of plants have to be present for the parasite to thrive. In *Devils Postpile* both hosts are commonly found but blister rust is not yet widespread this far south in the Sierra.

Western white pine does not occur in pure stands, but is scattered at elevations from 8000 to 9500 feet, especially in the Mammoth Lakes basin, usually with red fir trees (see below).

The other 5-needle pine commonly found in this quad is whitebark pine (*Pinus albicaulis*). This is *the* timberline species of the Sierra; it clings to windswept, rocky slopes to over 11,000 feet. Its whitish, flaky bark and its small, purplish cones—often broken open by Clark's nutcrackers to get the pine nuts—distinguish it from western white pine.

Whitebark pines generally look like trees according to the definition which says a tree has a "single main stem unbranched for several feet above the ground and a definite crown," etc. But often they appear to be prostrate, ground-hugging shrubs, due to high winds and deep, long-lasting snows. These elements of whitebark pine's environment force the tree into a horizontal growth form—known as *krummholz*—rather than the upright habit it is genetically programmed for. Any branches and buds which in some summers grow above the others on a plant and stick above the snow level are summarily killed the following winter by wind-blown particles of ice and snow. The plants therefore grow away from the wind, often along the ground, and often on the leeward side of a boulder. On barren summits, high winds blow most winter snow away before it melts into the ground. Hence, whitebark pines on high ridges are living under essentially arid conditions, and can be considered somewhat drought-resistant. Their ability to survive without much water is especially evident along the Deer Lakes Trail on Mammoth Crest.

Under crest-line conditions such as these, the tree grows very slowly, and past use of this species for firewood in subalpine regions has greatly depleted the amount of wood present. We recommend against the use of whitebark pine for fires, and standing dead trees especially should be left as they are because their esthetic qualities far outweigh their thermal values.

Low-growing *krummholz* pines on Mammoth Mountain

Fir trees are members of the pine family but are easily distinguished from the pines, and usually from each other. There are two firs in this part of the High Sierra.

California red fir (*Abies magnifica*) has flattened, four-sided needles, which are *not* grouped into fascicles on the branches. Another distinguishing characteristic of the species is its upright, barrel-shaped cones—up to 9″ long by 3″ in diameter—which disintegrate on the tree in the fall and are not found whole on the ground unless they have been cut by squirrels or blown down by high winds. The true firs are the only conifers in the Sierra that have upright cones. Red-fir bark is gray and thin on young trees, but red and thick, with deep furrows, on older specimens.

This species is not resistant to fire, especially when young, and it is absent where frequent ground fires favor the more resistant Jeffrey pine or the pioneering lodgepole pine. However, several decades without fire allow this tree to establish itself in the shade of less shade-tolerant plants, like the pines. Dense growths of young fir trees are a common sight under older pines, under aspens and under older firs.

Red fir is found up to 9,500 feet on most trails in *Devils Postpile* quad, and is especially common on the Iron Creek trail and on the slopes between Reds Meadow and Mammoth Pass.

White fir (*Abies concolor*) is a lower-elevation relative of red fir and is usually found below 8500 feet. We can easily tell mature white fir from mature red fir by its gray-brown, as opposed to reddish, bark. In addition, white fir cones are smaller than those of red fir, though they, too, disintegrate on the tree. Young fir trees are a bit more difficult to distinguish from each other. However, red-fir inner bark is invariably red, while that of white fir is not. Looking up through the crown of a white fir, we have a much more difficult time distinguishing individual needles and branchlets than we do on red fir, even on tall, old monarchs. Some people tell young white fir from

young red fir by looking closely at their needles: longer, and
twisted at the base in white fir, and appearing two-ranked
rather than sticking out all around the twigs as in red fir.

A delicate, wispy subalpine species is mountain hemlock
(*Tsuga mertensiana*). Found from about 8000 feet to timberline, it, like its associate whitebark pine, is often contorted
into *krummoholz* by the windy alpine environment.

The only plant mountain hemlock could possibly be
confused with is red fir. However, when the fir's single
needles break free of branches, they leave small, circular
scars, whereas peglike projections are left when the hemlock's
single needles are removed. Both have reddish bark, but that
of hemlock is usually flakier. From a distance we see that
mountain hemlock has a bent leader (tip) and a much more
pendulous, drooping appearance to its branches than red fir,
the limbs of which are more or less horizontal. Finally,
mountain hemlock has persistent cones 1-3″ long that hang
down, whereas red fir cones stick up.

Much of the mountain hemlock in our quad is near tree
line and stunted, but stands of good-sized trees occur on the
Beck Lakes loop above Johnston Meadow and just below
Summit Meadow. This is *not* the poison-hemlock Socrates
drank.

One broadleaf tree in the High Sierra is quaking aspen
(*Populus tremuloides*), of the willow family. This tree is
deciduous, losing all its leaves every autumn and growing a
new crop in spring. Its round-ovate leaves tremble in the
slightest breeze, hence the name. In the fall, before the leaves
drop, they become a delicate lemon yellow, which turns the
gullies and meadows that aspens inhabit into ribbons and seas
of gold. The sight is particularly pleasing to easterners who
miss the fall color of their native hardwood forests after
coming west. Aspen bark is white-to-greenish, becoming gray
and furrowed with age.

Although aspen ranges from Newfoundland to Alaska and

into Mexico, the species is not abundant in the Sierra. We can usually expect to see them along streams and in open, wet meadows, where their moisture requirements are most readily met. Like lodgepole pine, quaking aspen is shade-intolerant and has easily disseminated seeds (though most regeneration is by root-sprouts) so it, too, is a "pioneer" species which invades burns and meadows. Look for it above the North Fork of the San Joaquin on the trail from Corral Meadow to Twin Island Lakes, along which it is especially well established.

Aspens in Cascade Valley

The Fauna

OTHER GUIDES IN THIS SERIES have concentrated on the mammals of the High Sierra, but since birds are the most conspicuous animals in the high country— excepting, of course, mosquitos—let us here look at a few of the more abundant species of the Class *Aves*.

The most notable bird by far in *Devils Postpile* quadrangle is a member of the crow family: The Clark's nutcracker (*Nucifraga columbiana*). This bird is unmistakable. Usually heard before it is seen, it gives forth with a long, drawn-out, crowlike cry, "khr-a-a-a," as it swoops into the top of a whitebark pine tree to chip out a meal of pine nuts from the tree's closed cones (see *Flora*). The nutcracker's distinctive markings—gray body, black tail, and black wings with white patches—identify it in flight even at a distance. It is the only large bird so marked in the high country.

Not confined to a vegetarian diet, the Clark's nutcracker also acts as a predator, occasionally catching insects on the wing. It thus plays several roles in the timberline food web.

Everyone knows the American robin (*Turdus migratorius*), the most common member of the thrush subfamily in America. This bird is found from the tundra bordering the Arctic Ocean as far south as Guatemala at one time of the year or other. Most robins frequent *Devils Postpile* country during spring, summer and fall, though the author has sighted them high on Mammoth Mountain during a late winter blizzard.

A robin is not as boldly marked as a Clark's nutcracker, but its brick-orange breast—lighter in the female—and its erect stance as it runs about a meadow searching for food are unmistakable. The clear, caroling songs of males during early season, by which they mark out their nesting territories, are a welcome sound to mountain travelers.

After leaving their nest of mud, grasses and small twigs in the forking branches of a tree, young, spotted-breasted robins group together with adults and work their way to lower

elevations, where they feed largely on fruits and berries
during the winter. Robins are probably one of the few animals
that have become more abundant due to the changing face of
the earth. Our clearing of deep forests and our cultivating of
green lawns both increase this bird's habitat. In *Devils Postpile*
quad, robins are most often seen in meadows and along
streams where there are fruiting elderberry, currant and
gooseberry bushes.

Another member of the thrush subfamily, more often seen
than heard, is the mountain bluebird (*Sialia currucoides*).
Unlike other bluebirds, the mountain bluebird is really a blue
bird: it lacks the orange coloration of its lower elevation
cousins.

Its commonest habitats are alpine fell-fields above
timberline and meadows of the forest belt below 10,000 feet.
We watch for mountain bluebirds hovering in the air and
pursuing insects on the wing in the open country around
Thousand Island Lake and at Marie Lakes, near the John Muir
Trail. If the wind is still, we can hear their soft "chur" as they
flit lightly about their open mountain habitat.

A third member of the thrush subfamily we become familiar
with while hiking the wooded paths of *Devils Postpile*
quadrangle—this one more often heard than seen—is the
hermit thrush (*Catharus guttatus*). Adult hermit thrushes
have the characteristic spotted breast of the thrush subfamily
and a distinctive reddish tail which they slowly but
continually cock up and let down. However, our commonest
contact with this secretive bird is to hear the male's ethereal,
flutelike note echoing through the forest, from early to
midseason. His song consists of several distinct phrases each
introduced by a high, vibrant note, and is unlike any other
sound in the mountains. Hermit thrushes winter below the
deep-snow level on the lower slopes of the Sierra, but during
the summer they can usually be heard along the Muir Trail
near Upper Crater Meadow, among many other places.

The American dipper, or water ouzel (*Cinclus mexicanus*), is probably the most unusual bird the wilderness traveler will see in the Sierra. It is a permanent resident in and around mountain streams from the Aleutian Islands in Alaska all the way down to Panama. It remains all year round, as long as the water keeps flowing.

The dipper is the only bird one will see diving into a mountain stream and walking along the bottom. It is also the only songbird in the Sierra that commonly nests under waterfalls. This is the only avian of the High Sierra that sings year round. The chunky, slate-gray water ouzel was John Muir's favorite bird. *Devils Postpile* country visitors can expect to see water ouzels at Rainbow Falls and on Slide Creek near Hemlock Crossing, and indeed along most other permanent streams in the quadrangle.

Along with Clark's nutcrackers and robins, one is probably more likely to see a dark-eyed junco (*Junco hyemalis,* formerly called the Oregon junco) than any other bird in the High Sierra—if we don't include campgrounds and thus exclude the raucous Steller's jay.

Juncos resemble finches, and like them are mainly seed-eating birds, usually seen busily searching for food on the ground under trees and shrubs or out in open meadows. They are small birds with slate-gray heads, pinkish sides and striking white outer tail feathers, which flash in flight.

If you should suddenly be accosted by a loudly chirping junco—generally an extremely skittish bird—you can bet there is a well-lined, cuplike nest on the ground nearby which its owner would rather have remain unnoticed.

Dark-eyed juncos are found from the lowest reaches of the San Joaquin River through all forest types in the quad to alpine fell-fields, where at least some scattered dwarf willows exist for nest cover.

A true finch, and a bird of rather unusual habits, is the rosy finch (*Leucosticte arctoa*), which is a denizen of the highest peaks and snowfields of the quadrangle. This bird is unlikely to be confused with any other, for only rarely do any other feathered creatures, much less a similar-looking one, enter their alpine habitat.

Small flocks of these reddish, sparrow-sized birds can be seen through most of the year, feeding on seeds and insects that have blown from lower, more productive ecosystems onto glaciers and snowfields. Only in the severest winter storms do they appear to retreat downslope; they can be found at any time during the summer season high on the snow and talus of the Minarets, Mt. Ritter and Banner Peak, the highest points in the quadrangle.

For many years, a veteran wilderness hiker may not associate a thin "seet seet tseetle tseet" in dense fir forest with any animal in particular. Then one day as the hiker is strolling from 77 Corral toward Sheep Crossing, a flattish, brown-and-white bird about six inches long alights at the base of a large white fir just off the trail and starts spiraling up the trunk. "Seet seet tseetle tseet!" By golly! It's a brown creeper!

The high, wiry song of the brown creeper (*Certhia americana*) is not often noticed by Sierra travelers, but it is nearly always in the background when one is in heavy growth of red and white fir and Jeffrey pine in *Devils Postpile* quadrangle.

This common, inconspicuous little bird feeds almost exclusively on bark insects, using its tail as a brace in climbing *up* tree trunks. Woodpeckers normally work up tree trunks also, but they are much larger and noisier, and are usually predominantly black and white. Nuthatches are noisier and more colorful tree-stem foragers, and they usually go headfirst *down* a tree rather than up it.

Thus that squeaking song you've heard all these years, and that brown, mouselike creature flitting from tree trunk to tree trunk, are effect and cause: the brown creeper.

The Climate

CALIFORNIA'S WEATHER, and hence that of the Sierra Nevada, is governed by what goes on 2000 miles away, out over the Pacific Ocean. There, a permanent system of high pressure called the Pacific High moves north and south with the yearly march of the sun. In summer it is nearly due west of central California; in winter it lies off Baja.

When the Pacific High sits between the California coast and the subpolar low-pressure area in the Bering Sea during summer, it tends to keep the North Pacific's storms, bred in this low, from reaching the state. However, during the winter, the Pacific High is farther south, and also not as strong, while the subpolar low has increased in intensity. That's when storms move off the ocean over the land, and California gets rained on—or snowed on. Actually, it's not all that simple, but this brief sketch does help explain why about 53% of precipitation in *Devils Postpile* occurs in the winter, while only 3% comes during the summer, when most readers of this guide are likely to visit the mountains.

What about that 3%? This takes the form of short, summer-afternoon thunderstorms. When hot air from the Central Valley, or more rarely the Owens Valley, rises up the slopes of the Sierra, it cools at a rate of about 5.5°F per 1000 feet of altitude gain—the adiabatic rate of temperature change. In addition, the air over heat-radiating surfaces in the high country, such as an expanse of whitish granite, may rise convectively. Individually or together, these two phenomena cause the air to cool and drop its moisture. A thundershower is born. It "never rains in the Sierra in summer," but a cagoule or small tent is not that heavy—and wet sleeping bags aren't much fun.

Temperatures in the mountains vary with elevation. Generally, the temperature in stable air decreases by about 3.6° for every 1000-foot gain in elevation. So, a difference in temperature of 31°F can be expected between Miller

Crossing (4567'), on the San Joaquin in the southwest corner
of *Devils Postpile* quad, and the summit of Mt. Ritter
(13,157') due to the difference in elevation alone. The average
hiker is not likely to make this trip in one day, but the
possibilities are dramatic. When we add the chilling effect of
wind, a windless, 80° afternoon at Miller Crossing turns into
an experience of 30° on Ritter, assuming a 25-mile-per-hour
wind there. A windbreaker is another vital piece of summer
paraphernalia.

One last comment on climate: solar radiation reaching the
earth's surface increases with elevation. There may be four
times as much ultraviolet at 14,000' as at sea level, and
ultraviolet radiation causes sunburn. So visitors to the high
country who burn easily, or who haven't got a good tan by the
time they start living out in the sun, do well to liberally apply
zinc oxide or some other good ultraviolet screen—such as
a good ultraviolet screen with a sufficiently high SPF.
Sunglasses and a wide-brimmed hat may also be helpful to
hikers in the high country.

View west from Mammoth Crest

Backpackers

THERE ARE AS MANY REAsons for backpacking as there are backpackers. One of the most frequently cited reasons has something to do with "getting away from it all," and this usually means going where there aren't many other people.

It has been claimed that the density of humanity in the mountains varies inversely with the *square of the distance* from a road, and with the *cube of the elevation* above the road. To this might be added a third exponent: the density of humanity also varies inversely with the *fourth power of a route's "off-trail-ness,"* meaning the degree to which it is poorly marked or cross country. The hiker planning a trip in *Devils Postpile* can, by combining the trail descriptions and map in this volume, obtain a pretty fair idea of the probability of finding seclusion here.

The great increase in the use of the mountains for recreational pursuits has raised the question of just how many of us the land can handle. Overuse in *Devils Postpile* quad is evident in many places: the deeply eroded, multi-track pumice trails, especially near the Postpile; the nearly total lack of wood at the most popular campsites along the Muir Trail, such as Thousand Island Lake, Garnet Lake, Shadow Lake and Purple Lake; and accumulations of garbage and cans along Fish Creek. At various places in this guide, we recommend ways individual hikers can lessen their impact on the most heavily used areas—usually by camping someplace else and using a stove instead of wood fires. (Since the second edition of this book, in fact, we have left out all mention of firewood at the campsites described, to hopefully lessen the overuse of this dwindling resource.) However, some students and administrators of recreation areas foresee---in the not-too-distant future—a need even to close popular sites for a decade or more, so they can recover (as has been done, for example, on some islands of the Boundary Waters Canoe

Sign at Soda Springs Meadow

Area in Minnesota and in the *Devils Postpile* quadrangle at Shadow Lake, Garnet Lake and Thousand Island Lake, all near the Muir Trail.) This procedure would allow, among other things, compacted soil over suffocating tree roots to regain its porosity, and human wastes to decay and be recycled.

As well, a permit system has been instituted to limit the number of campers using those areas that have low capability of absorbing footsteps, dishwater and feces. Both the National Park Service and the U.S. Forest Service, which have the bulk of the jurisdiction over our wilderness areas and other wild places, have put together carefully thought-out rules that should help all of us who love the mountains to enjoy them without destroying their fragile beauty. We particularly encourage the use of only *existing* campsites greater than *100 feet* from trails and water; the disposal of wash water and burial of human wastes at *least 100 feet* from water, trails and campsites; use of *stoves* for cooking, not wood, and much smaller campfires; carrying out of *all* trash, *including* wet garbage; and respect for the solitude of these mountain cathedrals. The wild lands of North America are among the very last *hospitable* natural places on earth that have not been completely abused by humanity, technological as well as non-technological. It's their last stand, and ours. It's up to us.

The Trails

THE PROCLIVITY OF PEOPLE in our convenience society to let their amazing bodies atrophy while doing everything "the easy way" won't get them very far in the Sierra backcountry. You walk—or, more rarely, ride stock—or else you get nowhere. This is refreshing for the body as well as the soul. On those steep, dusty switchbacks, and in those cold, wet fords, there is a feeling of accomplishment and of sensuous contact with mother earth which no manufactured vehicle can give. Even calves sore from a long descent, or heels blistered on that extra five miles, are a small price to pay for the good-tired feeling, "Here I am, and I'm pooped, but I did it myself."

But walking need not be exhausting. The attractions of *Devils Postpile* quadrangle are made accessible to a wide variety of hikers by a system of trails we can divide into three basic categories: backpack trails, lateral trails and day-hike trails.

Backpack Trails. Backpack trails vary in length and difficulty from the 5½-mile jaunt into Deer Lakes to the 20½-mile John Muir Trail northbound from *Devils Postpile*. There are also intermediate length weekenders into remote lakes from easily reached trailheads.

Lateral Trails. Six lateral trails are described in this volume. They generally connect remote outposts, not normally visited by main-route travelers, to the backpack trails.

Day Hikes. A series of day hikes affords the visitor who is not inclined or able to take overnight trips quick access to scenic attractions that no one should miss seeing. Some trails may be walked in less than an hour, but remember, "this is not a place to make time but to spend it."

THE TRAILHEADS

Increasing vandalism to cars left at trailheads in the Sierra compels a few words of caution. Nothing of value should be left in sight in an unattended car, not even in a locked glove compartment or trunk, especially overnight. Thieves are primarily after wallets and purses with their cash and credit cards. Carry them with you or leave them at home. A car should, of course, be locked, and it should be left in as unremote a spot as possible for long backpacks. Devils Postpile National Monument is much better in this regard than Agnew Meadows, where several dozen vehicles have been burglarized on one night.

As of this writing, a shuttle bus operates between the Mammoth Mountain Ski Area parking lot and Reds Meadow during the summer months, in order to reduce traffic congestion and pollution in the San Joaquin River canyon. All travelers (with some exceptions) going into the Devils Postpile/Agnew Meadows/Reds Meadow area during the day must use the shuttle service, leaving their vehicles at the parking lot. This parking area is said to be relatively free of vandalism. Check with the Forest Service in Mammoth Lakes for current information on the status and costs of the shuttle-bus service.

Devils Postpile National Monument: 16 miles west of U.S. 395 through Mammoth Lakes on State Highway 203.

Reds Meadow: 17 miles west of U.S. 395 through Mammoth Lakes on State 203.

Agnew Meadows: 12 miles west of U.S. 395 through Mammoth Lakes on State 203.

Twin Lakes, Horseshoe Lake, Lake George: 6–8 miles west of U.S. 395 through Mammoth Lakes. Where State Highway 203 turns off for Mammoth Mountain and Devils Postpile, continue straight and follow the signs.

Granite Creek Campground (west-side access): From Oakhurst drive north and east to The Pines on Bass Lake. From here go 32 miles on Roads 434 (Beasore Road), 5S07 and 5S30 to the Granite Creek road, shortly beyond Clover Meadow. Follow it one mile to the campground.

Trail Descriptions

The route descriptions that follow often mention *ducks, cairns* and *blazes.* A duck is one or several small rocks placed upon a larger rock in such a way that the placement is obviously not natural. A cairn is a number of small rocks made into a pile. A blaze is a mark at eye level on a tree trunk made by removing a small section of the bark with an axe.

(Distances are one-way, unless otherwise indicated, and all map references are to the 1982 Wilderness Press edition of the *Devils Postpile* quadrangle.)

A note on water: There is increasing evidence of *Giardia* (an intestinal parasite) contamination of surface waters in the High Sierra, and the Forest Service and the Park Service are recommending that all drinking water from nontreated sources be boiled before use.

A last note: Be sure you have a wilderness permit—see **Introduction.**

DAY HIKE #1

Lake George to Lake Barrett and T.J. Lake (1½ mi. loop)

This short trip offers maximum high-country experience for a minimum of effort. It is recommended as a day hike for anyone who wants a beautiful but short hike. In addition, anglers will find Lake George and T.J. Lake loaded with rainbow trout.

Leaving the parking lot at the entrance to Lake George Campground (map section E3), we walk through the campground along the north shore of the lake to its bridged outlet. Our path crosses the stream in a growth of mountain alders and proceeds briefly along the shore of the lake below a cabin. After about 100 yards our signed route climbs upward to the left on loose, layered, metamorphic rock, past snowberry and pungent sagebrush. We cross a creek that has been flowing on our right and then continue ascending rather steeply on granite through a stand of mountain hemlock. Soon we arrive at quiet Lake Barrett.

The trail goes around the west side of the lake, but halfway along the shore we turn right, pass a stock trail that leads down toward Lake Mary, and climb over a low ridge to the shores of T.J. Lake. After such a brief walk from the road, one is amazed at the wild beauty of the place. Crystal Crag soars in the west, Mammoth Crest dominates the skyline to the south, and the northwest shore is bounded by steep granite walls. Lodgepole pines, western white pines and mountain hemlocks surround the lake, and a small meadow at the upper end is covered by wildflowers in mid season.

We can retrace our steps from here, or to complete a loop we can walk down the east side of the outlet stream on an umarked trail from T.J. Lake. Dropping steeply through the forest on this trail, we soon see Lake George below and Mammoth Mountain in the distance. Just above a cabin on the lake, our route cuts to the right and becomes a rough, wet fishermen's trail along the shore, through a thicket of willows and alders. When we emerge from the shrubbery, we are back where the trail begins to climb from Lake George.

DAY HIKE #2

Lake George to Crystal Lake (1 mi.)

Crystal Lake offers dramatic, high-country scenery and solitude for a minimum expenditure of time and energy.

From the parking area across from the entrance to Lake George Campground (map section E3), we proceed up the signed trail to Crystal Lake. This path takes us around the resort cabins above Lake George. The trail may be lost in the tract, but it becomes distinct again just below the top of the ridge directly behind the cabins, where it begins a southward traverse.

Crystal Lake and Crystal Crag

After climbing about ½ mile in deep pumice, we surmount the ridge and see a panorama extending from Banner Peak and Mt. Ritter in the west to Mammoth Mountain in the north and Gold Mountain and Coldwater Canyon in the east. We continue climbing to a signed fork where our route veers left (SE) and the main trail goes right (SW) to Mammoth Crest and Deer Lakes. Our trail climbs over a hump and then a profusion of trails drop through mountain hemlock and lodgepole and western white pine toward Crystal Lake. The lake is set dramatically at the base of granitic Crystal Crag, towering 700 feet above. Camping is possible on the east side and near the outlet, and there is a nice sandy beach at the upper end of the lake.

DAY HIKE #3

Twin Lakes to Mammoth Mountain Summit (3 mi.)

For vistas of the entire Mammoth Lakes basin and most of *Devils Postpile* quadrangle, the top of Mammoth Mountain is unexcelled. However, ski-area development on the mountain may turn some people off, and the hiker should be aware of nonesthetic roads and buildings at the top. (One is well-advised to dress warmly for this trek, because the west winds that roar almost constantly through Mammoth Pass can be devastating even on a warm summer day.)

Our signed trail leaves Twin Lakes campground between campsites 30 and 31 (map section E3). There is parking for 2–3 cars in a small space between sites 30 and 39, and also before the bridge crossing between the upper and lower lakes. Our route starts off steeply through scattered lodgepole pines and red firs with some aspens, the latter grotesquely bent by the deep winter snows that make Mammoth Mountain one of California's best ski areas.

Several hundred feet above Twin Lakes the trail begins to level off, and across a gully we soon pass a trail on the left.

We find some reddish porphyry here, a fine-grained volcanic rock containing some clearly seen crystals. This rock is a characteristic relic of Mammoth Mountain's days as an active volcano. Approaching the Bottomless Pit—a natural arch formed by erosion through a lava flow—we switchback steeply up through a brush field of manzanita, chinquapin, tobacco brush, rabbit brush and bitterbrush. Only occasional trees find a foothold in the shallow soil here. (Climbing in the Bottomless Pit is a danger, because of the steepness and loose rock, not only to the would-be climber but also to anyone down below at Twin Lakes, so the Forest Service has wisely closed the pit to hikers.)

From the pit we head west up a small draw about 50 yards, take the faint route forking to the right (the trail *ahead* contours west and south to McCloud Lake), and begin a rough, rocky ascent up the south side of the Dragons Back— the long, red, east flank of Mammoth Mountain—to Seven Lakes Point. When the sun is just right, one can see seven of the Mammoth lakes from here—Mary, George, Mamie, Horse-shoe, T. J. and Twin Lakes—as well as the White Mountains on the Nevada border, Crowley Lake in Long Valley, and Mammoth Crest.

From Seven Lakes Point we climb directly up the Dragons Back toward the summit, watching carefully for ducks, since the trail disappears and reappears several times along the ridge. The few stands of hemlock, lodgepole and whitebark pine along the path offer dramatic relief from the nearly incessant winds blowing from the west through Mammoth Pass. This pass is the low point on the Sierra crest through which winter storms come and dump several hundred inches of snow each winter in the Mammoth Lakes area. This blanket of snow not only delights skiers but also accounts for the magnificent forest of nearly pure Jeffrey pines found east of Highway 395 between Crowley Lake and Mono Lake—an area that would otherwise consist largely of sagebrush scrub.

As our climb continues, we can see this forest to the northeast, as well as Mono Lake, Mono Craters and the lookout on Bald Mountain. We also get glimpses of the ski lifts and maintenance roads on the east slope of the mountain. A few hundred feet below the summit, the barely perceptible sand-and-pumice trail peters out, but it is possible to continue upward on ski-area maintenance roads. The few wildflowers able to contend with the sandblasting on this slope consist mostly of various species of buckwheat. The few whitebark pines that have been able to get a foothold—usually on the leeward side of a rock—are more horizontal than vertical.

From the true summit—a little rise to the northwest across the summit depression—one has a 360° panorama.

DAY HIKE #4

Reds Meadow to Rainbow Falls (1 mi.)

Walter A. Starr, Jr., author of the well-known *Starr's Guide to the John Muir Trail,* called Rainbow Falls "the most beautiful in the Sierra outside of Yosemite." To reach this gem on the San Joaquin Middle Fork, we park at the end of the spur road that veers west from the Reds Meadow road about 200 yards north of the pack station, and start south down a wide, well-worn trail (map section D3).

After a short stroll under a cover of lodgepole pines, we cross in quick succession the combination John Muir Trail/Pacific Crest Trail southbound, a stock trail from Reds Meadow, and a riverside route from Devils Postpile, and continue to Boundary Creek (log bridge crossing). Shortly beyond the stream, the Fish Creek trail (Backpack Trail #6) continues on ahead, and we take the path to the right (west) for Rainbow Falls. The roar of the water fills our ears as we reach several vantage points for viewing and photographing the falls from the cliffs above the river. Early-season after-

Rainbow Falls   *Edwin Rockwell*

noons seem to be the best times to behold the falls with a
rainbow in full splendor. Interestingly, Rainbow Falls is cut-
ting down along a geologic contact that separates andesitic
rock to the south from rhyodacite rock to the north. The falls
has actually moved about 500 feet upstream to this point,
due to the river's eroding the softer rock strata at the base of
the falls. Look around at the bedrock here too; it shows many
good examples of glacial polish.

From the second viewpoint a steep stairway drops to the
river. Dippers—also called water ouzels—nest on the moss-
and-fern-covered walls beside the plunging water, and various
aquatic invertebrates line the rocks around the pool. Taking a
signed route from these viewpoints gets us a half mile farther
downstream to the Lower Falls.

DAY HIKE #5

Horseshoe Lake to Reds Meadow via Red Cones (6½ mi.) (Shuttle trip)

For hikers seeking a leisurely, mostly downhill jaunt
through the woods, views from one of the youngest volcanic
features in the region, and the chance for cold drinks and hot
baths at the end, this is the hike. A vehicle shuttle or
hitchhike is necessary, however, to get back to the trailhead.

At the end of the pavement and before the group campground at Horseshoe Lake, the Mammoth Pass trail (map section E3) takes off uphill through deep pumice under
lodgepole pines. We shortly reach a signed fork where a more
direct trail to Mammoth Pass and Reds Meadow goes right.

However, our route continues to the left (toward Red
Cones and McCloud Lake) and then forks again. We go left
(SW) toward the lake. We skirt the north side of the lake
through level pumice, climb a bit and then begin a barely perceptible descent—we have crossed the Sierra Crest and
entered the Ansel Adams Wilderness, though this is not
noted by signing. The runoff west of this summit is part of

the Great Valley drainage, which eventually runs into San Francisco Bay. The runoff to the east becomes part of the Owens River, most of which ends up—by *unnatural* means—in Los Angeles.

The trail begins to drop more steeply and then to switchback down, and the forest becomes more mixed as red fir, mountain hemlock and western white pine are added to the abundant lodgepole.

We soon descend to a fork near a sign for the John Muir Wilderness (which actually lies a half mile to the southeast). To the left is Upper Crater Meadow, and that fork meets the John Muir/Pacific Crest Trail there. But we turn right here, dropping toward the Red Cones and Reds Meadow. In another half mile, we arrive at another junction, this time with the former route of the John Muir Trail, and turn right. We go about 250 yards and then turn left (west) onto a signed trail to the top of the more northerly of the two Red Cones. The views are superb from the summit of this very young cinder cone (probably under 2000 years old), its youth evidenced by its lack of a pumice covering, though pumice blankets all the surrounding countryside.

From the summit of this cone, we retrace our steps to the last trail junction and turn left (north) onto the old John Muir Trail toward Reds Meadow. Our route drops slightly in red-fir forest and later rejoins the more direct trail between Mammoth Pass and Reds Meadow. We go left here and drop steeply on some long switchbacks for a mile to a trail fork. To the left (SW) a half mile away is Reds Meadow Resort and cold drinks. (Go right 100 yards through the stables where the trail ends to get to the store.) Ahead (NW) about ½ mile is Reds Meadow Campground with its hot springs and bathhouse. The choice is yours for the end of this hike—or you can have cold drinks and then stroll about ¼ mile north on a trail above the pasture to the bathhouse for a nice soak. (This trail is unmarked at the resort end, but is signed at the campground end. You can pick it up at the resort downhill from the store and past the lower cabins.)

DAY HIKE #6

Minaret Summit to Starkweather Lake (2½ mi.)
(Shuttle trip)

This trail is especially appealing if the shuttle bus service is still operating, since it allows a return to the start for free. Besides, it is an easy downhill hike past an old mine and several profusely flowered meadows just buzzing with hummingbirds in late season.

Our trail starts at a signed trailhead alongside the Minaret Summit Road just west of Minaret Summit (map section D2), and immediately begins dropping in deep pumice covered in season with mule ears, gilia, paintbrush, lupine and buckwheat. The trail soon enters red-fir forest and switchbacks past a cabin and some digs of the Minaret Mining Co. Beyond the cabin we continue to drop steadily, with occasional fine views through the trees toward the peaks of the Ritter Range to the west. About halfway down the slope, the trail begins to follow an abandoned road that parallels several streams and meadows with a profusion of wildflowers including monkshood, larkspur, lupine, corn lily and Indian paintbrush. Dozens of hummingbirds, especially rufous, are abundant along here in late season.

The trail switchbacks away from the last stream and meadow as the old roadbed it follows passes a stock trail heading north and approaches the Reds Meadow road just south of Starkweather Lake. Here the fishing is good, and the shuttle bus makes a stop at the north end. Be careful crossing the road!

"In wildness is the preservation of the world."
Henry David Thoreau

DAY HIKE #7

Agnew Meadows to Devils Postpile
via the Pacific Crest Trail (5 mi.) (Shuttle trip)

A segment of the Pacific Crest Trail goes south from
Agnew Meadows to Upper Crater Meadow, bypassing Devils
Postpile and Reds Meadow Resort. Part of this trail segment
also now serves as a stretch of the John Muir Trail. Following
is a description of a part of this trail southbound, which can
be followed for a delightfully pleasant day hike along a lovely
stretch of the Middle Fork San Joaquin River between Agnew
Meadows and Devils Postpile. (The shuttle bus, when operating, may be used to get from the end of this hike back to the
start if necessary.)

Exactly ¼ mile north from the road to Devils Postpile and
Reds Meadow, the road to Agnew Meadows reaches a parking
lot crossed by the PCT. Heading west from here (map section D2) on the marked trail, we come in 200 yards to
another parking area, on the south side of which we cross an
unnamed little stream on a log bridge. The sandy trail then
curves through a patch of lodgepole-pine forest and emerges
in a meadow that, in season, has a brilliant display of purple
whorled penstemon flowers. Here we recross the same stream
and then ascend slightly up a ravine, finding the PCT emblem
burned into boards. About 100 yards beyond signs welcoming us to the backcountry and to Ansel Adams Wilderness, our PCT route turns left toward the Middle Fork San
Joaquin River. On the open slope above the crashing river,
we can easily hear it during high runoff in early summer.

Well-engineered switchbacks lead down this slope past
scattered juniper trees to a junction about 100 yards from the
river and 70 vertical feet above it. From here a relatively
obscure connector trail leads upriver to the River Trail, which
goes on toward Shadow Lake and Thousand Island Lake. We
head down-canyon and quickly veer away from the river

under lodgepoles and red firs, with an understory of gooseberries and scarlet gilia. Soon we cross the Agnew Meadows stream in a lush setting of leafy alders, purple lupines, yellow senecios and white-trunked aspen trees. Beyond, the trail traverses above the river through pumice, with views of bald Mammoth Mountain down the canyon. About 1 mile from the last ford, we level off in a forest of pine and fir, then resume a moderate descent along which numerous trails of use lead down to picnicking, swimming and fishing spots beside the Middle Fork.

Now we bridge the river just upstream from Upper Soda Springs Campground and briefly make a climb among lodgepole pines and red firs. The trail veers rather far from the river, presently affords us views down on well-populated Pumice Flat and then crosses a little unmapped stream. From there we descend almost to the river, where it turns sharply from west to south. Soon a little ridge comes between us and the river, and we descend to a lodgepole-dotted pumice flat. In this flat we cross the several branches of Minaret Creek (difficult wade in early season) just below dramatic Minaret Falls. You may get

The base of Minaret Falls   *Thomas Winnett*

an excellent photo when the sun is above the top of the falls around noon.

Still in pumice, the trail overlooks the willowed meadows in which Minaret Creek and the Middle Fork wind down to their confluence, then veers away from both. Traveling momentarily west, we reach a junction from which the John Muir Trail, coming southeast from Shadow Lake, used to continue down to Devils Postpile, but now it has been rerouted southward from here on our recently built segment of the Pacific Crest Trail.

We'll be ending our hike at Devils Postpile, however, so we turn left here and descend on pumice under pine and fir along the former route of the John Muir Trail. Bypassing Soda Springs Meadow to our left, we soon pass a junction with the King Creek trail and in a few yards turn left across a footbridge over the Middle Fork just north of the buttresses of Devils Postpile itself. A quarter mile north of here on a well-beaten path is Monument headquarters and campground, where we end our walk.

BACKPACK TRAIL #1

John Muir Trail Northbound (20½ mi.)
(Devils Postpile National Monument to Donohue Pass)

This section of the John Muir Trail takes us along the east side of the Ritter Range through some of the most majestic scenery in the Sierra. Camping tends to be quite crowded on this route, and is now wisely restricted at the more scenic spots, such as Shadow Lake.

First we pick up the old Muir Trail near a bridge about ¼ mile south of the Devils Postpile National Monument parking

lot (map Section D3) and turn right, crossing the Middle Fork
San Joaquin River on the bridge.

After the Summit Meadow/77 Corral trail (Backpack Trail
#3) takes off to the left (south), we skirt the west edge of Soda
Spring Meadow, where many Belding's ground squirrels can
be seen. We soon enter a stand of lodgepole pine and red fir
and begin a steep ascent through deep, dusty pumice, shortly
meeting the rerouted combination John Muir/Pacific Crest
Trail coming in from the south. While the PCT northbound
heads off to the right, we continue climbing straight ahead,
now on the JMT. At the top of this climb, the trail levels off
shortly before Minaret Creek and passes the trail from Beck
Lakes (Backpack Trail #5). Minaret Creek can usually be
crossed on logs about 200 yards beyond this junction.

Our route, the Muir Trail, skirts the east side of Johnston
Meadow, which has a magnificent display of wildflowers into
midseason—and hordes of pollinating mosquitos. Where
we turn east from Johnston Meadow, the Minaret Lake trail
(Backpack Trail #4) continues west up the canyon of Minaret
Creek. Our path resumes climbing in dry, dusty pumice to tiny,
meadow-fringed Trinity Lakes. The Lois Lake trail takes off
west from our route a few yards north of the most southerly of
the Trinity Lakes, bound for Castle and Emily lakes. (These
two little lakes are excellent alternatives to camping at the
overused sites along the John Muir Trail. Both can be reached
in just one mile along this path. At first the trail is level in
lodgepole pine forest, and then it climbs northwest for ¼ mile
beside a spring-fed creek before turning north through
meadows and open forest to lovely Castle Lake. Emily Lake,
just beyond, offers even better camping. As of July 1981 the
trail did not continue to Lois Lake.)

From the Trinity Lakes the Muir Trail continues
northward, and after another short ascent we skirt the west
side of shallow Gladys Lake, where camping is uncrowded. A
ridge near the outlet affords views out over the San Joaquin

River canyon. To the west, the dark rocks of Volcanic Ridge dominate the skyline, and to the east the canyon walls drop away to the San Joaquin and rise on the far side to red-topped San Joaquin Mountain and the distinctive Two Teats.

From Gladys Lake we descend to a saddle, and then our path leads around the east side of Rosalie Lake to good campsites on that shore. From this lake the trail goes through a gap and drops in heavy forest via a long series of switchbacks to beautiful Shadow Lake, once a true gem of the mountains. Camping here is now poor, and is heavily restricted due to crowds and site degradation. This is one place along the John Muir Trail that is really being worn out. The soil over tree roots around the lake is being badly compacted—which contributes to root disease and tree death—and firewood is not to be found. Currently, camping and fires are wisely prohibited by the Forest Service along the north shore of the lake. Therefore, to conserve the fragile beauty of Shadow Lake, we recommend that travelers not camp here at all but stop at Rosalie Lake or continue up Shadow Creek, even though creekside campsites there are suffering from heavy camping pressure too and restrictions are in effect.

After crossing the inlet of Shadow Lake, the Muir Trail joins the Ediza Lake trail (Backpack Trail #7) and ascends westward with it for about one mile through Shadow Creek canyon before branching north. This trail section suffers heavy use and is likely to be dusty, particularly in late season. However, the dust is behind us after the trail emerges from forest cover and completes the 1000-foot climb from Shadow Creek to the rocky ridge above Garnet Lake. This ridge is an excellent place from which to appreciate the view of the lake itself, and Mt. Ritter, Banner Peak and Mt. Davis in the west. The traveler will also note the striking change in the countryside. From the heavily timbered slopes of Shadow Creek canyon, we have entered a landscape which, except for scattered stands of stunted hemlock and lodgepole pine, is predominantly glacially polished rock.

From this viewpoint the trail descends 400 vertical feet to the outlet of Garnet Lake. (An unsigned lateral leading to the River Trail branches from our route just before the outlet of Garnet Lake. It passes south of the rock outcrop beside the outlet and then drops very steeply through a notch into pine and hemlock forest, where it switchbacks to a crossing of the Middle Fork and a junction with the River Trail-Backpack Trail #8.) Camping is not allowed near the outlet and is only fair on the north side of the lake, but there are several nice, as well as legal, sites on the south shore.

Beyond the outlet of Garnet Lake we cross the talus-covered 500-foot ridge that separates Garnet and Thousand Island lakes. En route, the trail circles the east shore of dramatic Ruby Lake, and then drops down past colorful Emerald Lake. Both of these lakes offer fine camping. Then we descend to the outlet of Thousand Island Lake, whose island-dotted surface reflects the imposing facade of Banner Peak and the sharply etched mass of Mt. Ritter. Several exposed campsites, subject to a great deal of wind coming down from Glacier Pass, may be found on the north and south sides of the lake. No camping is allowed near the outlet, just north of which we pass the terminus of the two trails from Agnew Meadows (Backpack Trails #8 and #9) and then climb northwest away from the lake and onto a ridge. Along this ridge the hiker in the right season will discover a verdant growth of wildflowers including lupine, sulfur flower, Mariposa lily, goldenrod, fleabane, mountain aster, streptanthus, elephant heads and pussy paws.

On this ridge the trail levels off for a while through lodgepole and hemlock, and then it emerges from tree cover to the meadows and ponds of Island Pass, where fairy shrimp and mountain frogs—as well as mosquitoes—are abundant from early to mid season. Camping is adequate here until the water stops flowing in mid season. From Island Pass we drop steadily northwest through forest cover and arrive at Rush Creek Forks, where camping is crowded.

Jeff Schaffer

1000 Island Lake, Banner Peak and Glacier Pass

Beyond the forks our route soon passes the Rush Creek
trail. (This trail crosses several tributaries of Rush Creek and
descends in less than a mile to the north shore of Waugh Lake,
with numerous campsites along the way. Below the dammed
outlet of the lake, a steep switchbacking trail climbs south
about 600 vertical feet to scenic Weber Lake, where there are
several nice campsites among severely glaciated metamorphic
rocks. Below the Weber Lake trail junction, the Rush Creek

trail drops to Lower Rush Meadow. From the signed junction here, one can proceed downstream to a crossing of Rush Creek and follow a trail to Clark Lakes, or turn left to Gem and June Lakes.)

Beyond the Rush Creek Trail we ascend steeply through a thinning forest cover to the trail to Marie Lakes (Lateral Trail #4). From just north of this junction up to Donohue Pass, the John Muir Trail crosses the southwest corner of *Mono Craters* quadrangle. Leaving forest cover, the trail winds up through boulder-dotted, stream-laced meadows and then climbs via rocky switchbacks to Donohue Pass on the Sierra crest. Vantage points near this pass afford great views of the Sierra crest, the Cathedral Range, the Ritter Range and Lyell Canyon. (For the trail from here north, see the High Sierra Hiking Guide to *Tuolumne Meadows.*)

BACKPACK TRAIL #2

John Muir Trail Southbound (11 mi.)
(Devils Postpile National Monument to map's edge)

The John Muir Trail southbound from Devils Postpile tours a fascinating part of the Mammoth area's volcanic formations and then enters the granitic high country to the south. From the main parking lot (map section D3) our route leads south toward Devils Postpile through a large meadow in which the Middle Fork San Joaquin River meanders. In mid season this meadow is a sea of lavender shooting stars, showy flowers that inhabit wet meadows throughout the quadrangle. At the south end of the meadow we step onto a superannuated section of the famous John Muir Trail. This trail has recently been rerouted west of the river through the Monument. We'll pick up a recently built section of the Muir Trail south of the Devils Postpile. (Actually, one can save about two miles of

Polished top of Devils Postpile

walking by beginning this hike at the Fish Creek trailhead near Reds Meadow. But if you do that, you won't see the Postpile.)

Our well-packed pumice trail passes beneath the pillars of the Devils Postpile, and a highly recommended side trail leads to the top. Beyond the Postpile, the hiker encounters a profusion of tracks in the easily disturbed pumice. One should stay on the most heavily used and blazed route, and watch for signs. The trail is gently rolling here, through a forest of lodgepole pine, red fir and Jeffrey pine, with few vistas to relieve the monotony of the trees.

We shortly pass one trail going left (east) toward Reds Meadow, and after a gentle 1½-mile stroll from the start we reach a signed junction with a section of the combination John Muir/Pacific Crest Trail and turn left onto it. Our route swings in and out of several drainages as we climb gently eastward in open forest of Jeffrey pine and red and white fir.

We soon cross several trails and a road leading south from the Reds Meadow area toward Rainbow Falls and Cascade Valley. A profusion of colorful flowers, especially in the wetter areas, lines the trail here with lupine, larkspur, paintbrush and monkey flower being among the many species present.

After fording numerous streamlets and then substantial, 4-channeled Boundary Creek, we make a serious climb on long switchbacks between Boundary and Crater creeks. These take us under heavy cover of red fir to a log crossing of Crater Creek, where we leave Ansel Adams Wilderness and enter John Muir Wilderness. Camping is good here, but watch out for mosquitoes and bears.

The trail continues on toward Upper Crater Meadow by climbing between the geologically young Red Cones, recrossing Crater Creek and passing an abandoned section of the John Muir Trail leading off to the north.

Our route then reaches Upper Crater Meadow, where the deeply rutted trail ought to be rerouted because of vegetation damage. Here, where a trail comes in from Mammoth Pass, Belding's ground squirrels keep the soil loose with their burrowing, and lodgepole pines are invading the grasses along the meadow's edge. A long, gentle climb takes us to a long meadow from where we can see The Thumb to the northeast. A profusion of streamlets and springs lines this section of the trail into mid season, so there is the possibility of camping here when the more popular sites along the trail are taken. Along this stretch we often hear the raucous call of Clark's nutcrackers, as well as the ethereal tune of the hermit thrush. Soon we cross a low divide and begin to drop toward Deer Creek on a dry, south-facing slope covered with sagebrush, Indian paintbrush, chinquapin, manzanita and gooseberry. Here we get our first views of vast Cascade Valley and the Silver Divide beyond.

Camping is good at Deer Creek. Leaving here, one is wise to carry water for the next three miles, which are dry, dusty, and up. During late season one might not encounter water again until Duck Creek, 5 uphill miles ahead. On this long traverse through open lodgepole pine above Fish Creek the footing ranges from pumice to granite sand, and we have

Cascade Valley

increasingly revealing views up glaciated, U-shaped Cascade Valley and to the Silver Divide. (About halfway between Deer and Duck creeks we leave *Devils Postpile* quadrangle and enter the southwest corner of *Mt. Morrison.* For a description of the trail from here, the reader is referred to the Wilderness Press *Guide to the John Muir Trail.*)

BACKPACK TRAIL #3

Devils Postpile to Granite Creek (17½ mi.) (shuttle trip)

This trail over the Ritter Range follows a part of the old Mammoth Trail, which prospectors and stockmen used in the late 19th Century to cross the mountains between Clover Meadow and Reds Meadow. It offers the easiest access to the little-used North Fork country and takes us from an eastside roadend (Devils Postpile) to a westside one (Granite Creek). This spectacular area was only recently afforded statutory protection when it was incorporated into the expanded and renamed Ansel Adams Wilderness.

To get on the trail, we walk through the meadow south of the parking lot at Devils Postpile National Monument (map section D3) and turn right to cross a bridge over the Middle Fork San Joaquin River. (Note the carbonated—and tasty—soda spring at the meadow's edge.) Then in 50 yards we turn left (south) at the first trail junction and begin a climb through lodgepole pine in deep, dusty pumice. Along this ascent we have a nice overview across the San Joaquin to the basalt buttresses of Devils Postpile, which formed when molten lava cooled to fracture into long, straight-sided columns less than 100,000 years ago. We shortly cross the combined John Muir/Pacific Crest Trail, and after the first switchback Mammoth Mountain and the Red Cones come into sight through scattered red and white firs, mixed with western white pines. Soon after leaving the Monument and entering Inyo National Forest and Ansel Adams Wilderness, we descend through a forest of scattered firs and pines to King Creek. Take a sniff of the strongly scented bark of a large Jeffrey pine: is it vanilla or root beer?

In early and mid season the observant hiker is likely to see the brilliant red snow plant here. A member of the wintergreen family, it is a flowering plant that lacks chlorophyll and hence cannot carry on photosynthesis. It lives on organic matter in the soil.

King Creek offers good camping and yields up small rainbow trout (6-8″) to anglers. An easy crossing can usually be made on logs downstream below the ford or on boulders upstream; then the uphill grind to Summit Meadow begins. We gradually leave the fairly dense cover of trees and come out onto a dry granite slope covered with manzanita and huckleberry oak. While stopping for a breather on one of the many switchbacks, the hiker has a panoramic vista to the east and south, from Mammoth Mountain to the Silver Divide. Wild strawberries, Indian paintbrush and red-flowered mountain pride may be seen along the trail here.

From this dry slope we begin climbing steeply into a denser north-slope forest of mountain hemlock as the Minarets appear in the north. About ⅓ mile below Summit Meadow, the Summit Meadow cutoff to upper King Creek leads off to the

right. We turn left here and climb 300 feet to the former
meadow, which was used for summer sheep grazing until 1963.
It has since become almost totally covered with lodgepole
pines, a pioneer species which at this elevation in the Sierra is
the next step after a meadow in ecological succession (see the
chapter "Flora"). The trampling and grazing of sheep
apparently kept the meadow from turning into forest while
grazing continued, but when the Forest Service limited
sheepherding to the west side of the North Fork San Joaquin,

Summit Meadow in 1981

the broken ground here in the meadow was an ideal place for seeds from the surrounding lodgepole-pine forest to germinate and carry on the natural process of succession.

Climbing beyond Summit Meadow—which is neither a meadow nor at the summit—we enter a dense stand of lodgepole pine and red fir. After entering Sierra National Forest at the top of Granite Strairway, we drop steeply on rocky granite footing to the base of Granite Stairway, leaving Inyo's pumice behind for good. Seasonal blooms such as penstemon and lupine delight the eye as we level off and arrive at Stairway Creek. We continue downhill to Lower Stairway Meadow, which in mid season is covered with nodding lavender shooting stars. Some of the common summer birds seen along the trail at this elevation are brown creepers, white- and red-breasted nuthatches, kinglets and Steller's jays.

After a short climb out of Lower Stairway Meadow, the trail levels off through red-fir and lodgepole-pine forest, and we get our first glimpses of the Isberg Pass country to the northwest. Soon, however, our route begins a steep, switchbacking descent into Cargyle Meadow, down the west slope of a glacial moraine which is a riot of wildflower color in mid season during wet years. Numerous seeps dotting the hillside nourish forget-me-not, elderberry, pennyroyal, Indian paintbrush, cranesbill, lupine, monkey flower and scrub willow. Cargyle Meadow, which we circle to the south before crossing East Fork Cargyle Creek, is itself a sea of blooms in season—shooting star, knotweed, wild strawberry and Labrador tea. On the north side of Cargyle Meadow, polished granite bedrock evinces the scraping power of the glaciers that passed here over 10,000 years ago.

Our route crosses the creek, where camping is fair, then climbs over a rise and drops to Corral Meadow, also called 77 Corral. During the drought of 1877, this was one of the pastures in the Sierra heavily used by sheepmen—hence the signed designation *77 Corral*. From 77 Corral, where there are several packer campsites, trails lead to Iron Lake, Iron Creek, and Hemlock Crossing.

Our route crosses the meadow to the southwest and drops steadily toward West Fork Cargyle Creek through cathedral groves of white fir and Jeffrey pine. Scattered clumps of bitter cherry, with their mid-season blossoms or late-season delicately yellow-tinted leaves trembling in the breeze, also delight the nose and the eye. Beyond the stream, in an area where you may encounter mule deer, the trail forks in Snake Meadow. The right branch goes northwest toward Iron Creek, but we continue southwest and in a few hundred yards begin descending earnestly on switchbacks under a cover of dry, open forest toward Sheep Crossing on North Fork San Joaquin River. This west-facing slope gets the direct rays of the afternoon sun, so we see a predominance of black oak, Jeffrey pine, manzanita and huckleberry oak—all characteristic of drier sites and lower elevations. Past a side trail (Lateral Trail #6) to the Middle Fork San Joaquin River, we drop the final 400 feet to Sheep Crossing.

At Sheep Crossing—used by sheepherders to bring their flocks across the river until 1963—the trail crosses on a recently rebuilt bridge and jogs south ¼ mile before beginning a steep ascent up the west wall of the canyon.

The rigors of this 1600-foot climb are ameliorated somewhat by its location on a relatively cool east-facing slope covered with a variety of shade-producing trees including sugar pine, white fir, incense-cedar, black oak and Jeffrey pine. Numerous streamlets and seeps in season nourish a variety of herbs, too, including orange Sierra lily, red-and-yellow columbine and lavender shooting star. Even occasional azaleas, covered with white blossoms in early season, perfume the air as we climb through this delightfully varied forest.

As our trail levels off at the end of its ascent from the river, it soon widens into a road, and we find ourselves out of the wilderness. Behind us is a final view of the Ritter Range and the North Fork Canyon. From saddle 7527, midway along a crest connecting Green and Cattle mountains, we enter an area that was being logged in 1989. The roads are currently in disarray here, so check with the Forest Service for up-to-date road information. One should, however, be able to make a generally descending trek west for 3 miles on Forest Service Road 4S57 to Granite Creek Campground, which is the closest roadend easily reachable by conventional vehicles, where our hike ends.

BACKPACK TRAIL #4

Devils Postpile to Minaret Lake (6½ mi.)

Minaret Lake affords some of the finest closeups of the stark and jagged Minarets that can be had on a weekend trip. To get there, we take the John Muir Trail northbound (Backpack Trail #1) from Devils Postpile National Monument to Johnston Meadow. Then, where the Muir Trail turns east, we continue upstream to the northwest. Our trail climbs in pumice through a forest of red fir, western white pine, lodgepole pine and mountain hemlock, and then breaks out onto a granite slope, where it switchbacks up beside the cascades of Minaret Creek. As we labor up the switchbacks, we get increasingly better views of the marvelous Minarets.

After leveling out, our path passes some old road segments associated with the Minaret Mine (operated 1928-1930). From here, ½ mile of level walking beside the meandering stream brings us to good campsites. The silent early-morning riser is apt to see browsing Inyo mule deer in these meadows. From the campsites, several steep ascents take us through the last timber stands before laboring up some rocky switchbacks to Minaret Lake. Dramatic campsites dot the northern, eastern and southern shores.

Settled beside this inspiring lake, one looks with awe on the towering array of aretes to the south and west. These knife-edge ridges are remnants of ancestral mountains that existed more than one hundred million years before the present Sierra was uplifted. Glacial plucking at their bases and frost wedging in their cracks and joints have determined their striking relief. Minaret Lake is often used as a base camp for "technical" climbing in the Minarets. Experienced back-packers may want to continue on around the north shore of the lake and take the difficult ducked route up to Cecile and Iceberg lakes, where the scenery is even more spectacular.

BACKPACK TRAIL #5

Beck Lakes Loop (Devils Postpile to Beck Lakes via King Creek, Fern Lake and Holcomb Lake) (18 mi. loop)

This loop trip takes us in a long, clockwise circle from Devils Postpile National Monument to King Creek, Fern Lake, Holcomb Lake, Beck Cabin and Beck Lakes, and back again to the Postpile. It tours a popular area heavily used by packers and groups. The loop may be walked in either direction. Doing it clockwise avoids 5 uphill miles of deep pumice between the Postpile and Beck Cabin. Doing it counterclockwise gets most of the uphill out of the way on a shaded north-facing slope. The route is here described in a clockwise direction.

The first 6 miles of this trail, to the cutoff below Summit Meadow, are described in Backpack Trail #3. Just before Summit Meadow, we leave the Devils Postpile/Granite Creek trail and head north for Beck Lakes. After a long haul from King Creek, this trail is a welcome gentle stretch through swales of willow, elderberry and corn lily, and dense stands of

Left: Minaret Lake and Minarets

mountain hemlock. After ½ mile we crest a minor ridge
and come to the lateral trail to Fern Lake. This almost level
short trail follows the south bank of the outlet stream to good
campsites all around the lake. There is a nice sandy beach on
the southwest corner of the lake. (For more secluded camping,
experienced backpackers may go cross country northwest ¾
mile through a gap to Anona Lake.)

Continuing beyond the Fern Lake lateral on the main trail,
we pass several wet meadows and seasonal ponds and then
descend to the outlet stream of Anona Lake near its junction
with King Creek. We cross the several branches of Anona
Lake's outlet fairly easily, and then swing up to the west before
switchbacking across the open granitic slope west of cascading
King Creek. Watch for blazes on the scattered lodgepoles.
Now we climb steeply toward King Creek, with views back
toward Mammoth Crest and the Silver Divide, and then drop
to a cold ford, which is much easier to negotiate in late season
when the water is lower. Our route soon intersects the
Holcomb Lake trail, which we take to the left at a mosquito-
infested meadow.

The Holcomb Lake trail was being rerouted in 1981,
presumably to make it easier for packer groups to get to the
lake, which is very popular for day rides out of Reds Meadow.
The new route climbs west across open granitic rocks above
the combined outlet streams of Holcomb and Ashley lakes,
veers north and passes small, warm Noname Lake. Beyond
this lake we pass some ponds and then arrive at Holcomb
Lake. Campsites are scattered around the lake, which has
some nice diving rocks. During early and mid season, willow
thickets around the lake offer nesting and feeding cover and
song perches for the natty, distinctively marked white-crowned
sparrow, a summer resident in most of the High Sierra that
adds much to one's wilderness experience.

Nearby Ashley Lake, at the base of Iron Mountain, has no
trail to it. This is perhaps fortunate, since it is a more dramatic

spot than Holcomb Lake, and the absence of a trail helps keep
the crowds out. A short cross-country ramble by experienced
backpackers up either side of the Ashley Lake outlet (stay *near*
the stream!) under mountain hemlock and whitebark pine and
through meadows brings one to the lake. Campsites are scarce,
but Iron Mountain and its glacier looming above make this a
much more scenic spot than Holcomb Lake. It's quieter also.
Iron Mountain is easily climbed from Ashley Lake (see *A
Climber's Guide to the High Sierra.*)

Back at the mosquitoey junction we hurry on to Beck
Cabin, built by an early prospector in this area and now
dilapidated. The Beck Lakes trail takes off to the north at a
sign near the cabin and passes some wet meadows, dotted with
turpentine-scented Labrador tea and pink-blossomed bog

Holcomb Lake *Jeff Schaffer*

laurel, on the way to Superior Lake. Several campsites near
the lake's inlet and outlet offer fair-to-good camping and
swimming once the mosquitoes are gone. Beyond Superior
Lake the path can be difficult to follow in early season, due to
deep snows on the shady and wooded northeast slopes. It is
best to stay above and left of the stream as the route skirts the
south side of a meadow upstream from Superior Lake and
ascends steeply through wet meadows and open stands of
mountain hemlock.

Our path crosses the outlet stream of the lower lake just
above a grove of mountain hemlock, and from the ford we
follow the ducked and rocky route to Lower Beck Lake.
Camping is stark but scenic on the north shore of the lower
lake and south of the outlet. A faint, rocky trail along the north
side of the lower lake leads to remote Upper Beck Lake, which
is quite barren save for some stunted alpine vegetation. Red-
tinted green algae color lingering snowbanks here throughout
the summer.

To complete our loop, we backtrack to Beck Cabin and,
regaining the main trail, climb east across a slope dotted with
western white pine, red fir and pinemat manzanita. The
dramatic vista ahead includes the Silver Divide, the Middle
Fork San Joaquin canyon and Snow Canyon, and looking back
we have a last glimpse of Iron Mountain and the south end of
the Ritter Range. Now we cross the crest of the ridge we've
been climbing, circle a wet meadow, and then climb once again
through mixed forest. After this short, steep ascent, the trail
to the Postpile is generally downhill in ever-deepening, dry,
dusty pumice, which makes the hiker now appreciate this
direction of the loop.

Long, switchbacks soon bring us out above Johnston Lake
and Johnston Meadow, about 500 feet below. On this
relatively cool and shady north slope, the tree cover is made
up of shade-tolerant red fir and mountain hemlock. On this
steep slope the typical tree trunk has a curve near the ground.

Deep, heavy snowpacks bent the trees as seedlings and saplings; then, after they grew large enough to resist this force and stay upright during the winter, the bases remained deformed.

After a long descent, we approach Minaret Creek and Falls, and meet the Muir Trail, which we follow south. In a half mile, where the Muir Trail joins the Pacific Crest Trail going south, we head east, following signs back to Devils Postpile.

BACKPACK TRAIL #6

Reds Meadow to Fish Creek and Cascade Valley (16 mi.)

The Fish Creek-Cascade Valley trail is the primary pack-train route out of Reds Meadow, and it tends to be crowded and dusty. However, it leads to good fishing, hot springs, and a glaciated canyon that to some eyes resembles Little Yosemite Valley.

We walk south from the trailhead parking lot near Reds Meadow, as described in Day Hike #4, but at the Rainbow Falls turnoff, we continue south on the Fish Creek trail, under a canopy of pine and fir. Compared to most of the trails in the quadrangle, this one passes through areas of relatively low elevation, where we see plants not encountered in the Devils Postpile high country, such as incense-cedar and black oak. The path is nearly level here, but wide and deep through dusty, easily disturbed pumice. We then drop to Crater Creek, and stroll along with refreshing riparian vegetation on our left and dry pine forest on our right.

The crossing of Crater Creek is best made about 10 yards upstream on two rotting logs in a dense growth of alders. Continuing beyond the crossing, one notices again the great difference in environments between streamside and dry hillside. Along the creek are dense growths of alder, bracken, willow and currant, and such wildflowers as orange Sierra lily, 6-foot-tall cow parsnip and both pink and yellow monkey flowers. Out in the pumice, however, away from the immediate vicinity of the stream are more drought-resistant species: scattered Jeffrey pines and red and white firs, with manzanita the predominant shrub. After the trail crosses an unnamed stream, we come onto a granite slope which in early season is overrun with hundreds of snowmelt rills. This slope is an excellent example of what the ecologist calls "primary succession": a new surface, never covered by plant life previously, is being overlaid with vegetation. Both meltwater from winter snows and weathered rock are allowing alders, willows and other pioneer plants to get a shallow foothold on the otherwise bare rock (see the chapter "Flora"). The trail is blasted out of the granite in places; we have left the pumice behind. Near the ford of Cold Creek is a worn-out campsite. From here our route climbs first through aspen and then through a stand of large Jeffrey pine, incense-cedar and white fir, with a few black oaks scattered around. At the end of this climb, we cross a divide and begin dropping, at first gently and then steeply down switchbacks, into Fish Valley. Silver Creek is visible south across the canyon. Lower-elevation black oak and incense-cedar are becoming more frequent as we descend, and mosquitoes are rare on this dry, south-facing slope. Two thirds of the way down, the trail grades into a long, gentle, descending, eastward traverse, passes the washed-out and abandoned bridge site, and ends ⅓ mile past it at Island Crossing. There are heavily used fishermen's camps here. More secluded accommodations can be found both upstream and downstream, where fallen trees offer dry crossings.

After bridging the main stream, we quickly arrive at a fork in the trail. To the right and heading back downstream is the little-used Silver Creek trail. (This route climbs in aspen around the wet meadows just downstream from here and circles back to Fish Creek at the old bridge site. Then it turns south and begins more than a mile of steep switchbacks, first beside an unnamed tributary and then across waterless slopes, till it levels out and completes an 1800-foot ascent by traversing over to Silver Creek and a trail junction. One trail from here heads south toward Margaret Lake and Mono Hot Springs in the *Mt. Abbot* quadrangle, while the other heads west toward String Meadows, an area mostly noted for its fresh cowpies.)

But we go left, and as we head up Fish Valley, open Jeffrey-pine groves with sagebrush and lupine underneath alternate with dense stands of white fir and incense-cedar. About 1½ miles upstream, Fish Creek makes a sharp bend north and our path continues beside Sharktooth Creek through cool, green stands of alder, azalea, elderberry, currant and gooseberry nourished by runoff rills. In early season the

Fish Creek in Cascade Valley

fragrance of swamp onion wrinkles the nose of the hiker who steps on it when leaving the trail to skirt numerous flooded spots. We pass several heavily used packer campsites along the stream and go by the Sharktooth trail, which switchbacks south off the quadrangle in the vicinity of Lost Keys Lakes. We then cross Sharktooth Creek to Iva Bell Camp, which is even more heavily used and is not uncommonly littered with dog-food cans and beer cans. (Fish Creek, or Iva Bell, Hot Springs are about 100 yards up the path that goes through this campsite. There were three relatively clean and usable pools there when checked by the author in 1981. Let's keep them that way—NO SOAP, PLEASE!)

From Iva Bell Camp we make a steep 700-foot climb over a chaparral-covered ridge and then descend to Fish Creek again. The stream drops fast here between glacially polished walls of granite, and the trail occasionally climbs around rock outcrops on its way to Second Crossing. In mid season this stretch of trail is a riot of wildflower blooms: paintbrush, penstemon, forget-me-not, wallflower, gilia and Mariposa lily are all evident. Fording at Second Crossing is easy only in late season. Above Second Crossing, Jeffrey pine, lodgepole pine and juniper alternate with black cottonwood and aspen along the stream. Many lovely pools offer fine opportunities for both swimming and fishing along this section of the creek. Across from the outlet stream of middle Lost Keys Lake we leave *Devils Postpile* quad and enter *Mt. Morrison*. After another mile our path crosses the several distributaries of Duck Creek, then climbs south over a little ridge before finally dropping to the flats of Cascade Valley.

Cascade Valley is a steep-sided, flat-bottomed valley which was gouged out by glaciers originating at the Sierra crest over 10,000 years ago. The valley gets its name from the cascades of tributary streams, such as Purple Creek, Long Canyon and Minnow Creek, which were left hanging when the glacier deepened the main valley more than the side canyons.

Fish Creek meanders here in what was once possibly the bed of a glacial lake, formed behind a recessional moraine of the Fish Creek glacier. As we stroll through the lodgepole pine stands interspersed with meadows, we may see the rare black-backed three toed woodpecker, as well as the commoner robin, the dark-eyed junco, and the scolding winter wren.

Numerous pack-train trips terminate in Cascade Valley; it is a popular stopping point for travelers passing through, and in summer there often is a Forest Service wilderness ranger near Purple Creek, so one is seldom alone in this place—and that's another way that it resembles Little Yosemite Valley. After the Minnow Creek trail leaves our path, and the steep path to Purple Lake takes off to the north, the Fish Creek trail continues upstream a mile to Third Crossing. (This description is continued in the High Sierra Hiking Guide to *Mt. Abbot*.)

BACKPACK TRAIL #7
Agnew Meadows to Ediza Lake (6½ mi.)

This trail leads to the spectacular Ritter Range, capped by Banner Peak, Mt. Ritter and the Minarets. Some say the alpine beauty of all Sierra lakes culminates at Ediza Lake, where amid towering evidences of glacial and mountain-building action, the visitor can readily appreciate the colossal forces that shaped these natural landforms. Scaling most of the peaks hereabouts requires technical rock-climbing experience, and hikers who have not had such experience should not attempt them without the guidance of capable climbers.

Our signed route leaves the south side of the second parking lot just beyond Agnew Meadows Pack Station (map section D2). As we head west, our route passes a fenced pasture, and we jump several streamlets under lodgepole pine before passing a sign welcoming us to Ansel Adams Wilderness and arriving at a fork. Here we continue straight ahead

(NW) as the PCT turns left toward Devils Postpile and Reds Meadow, descend a dry slope covered with chaparral, and pass an unmarked trail connecting with the PCT to the left. Then our route skirts the northeast shore of shallow Olaine Lake, and just beyond the lake turns west, leaving the River Trail. Passing through aspen and sagebrush, we arrive at a bridged crossing of the river. Beyond, we jog south a bit and then begin our climb.

The trail up the west side of the canyon is rocky but well-manitained. This path rises steeply for 800 feet up juniper-dotted sagebrush slopes on switchbacks, and the hiker is rewarded by excellent views of cascading Shadow Creek as it falls from the lip of Shadow Lake's outlet. Hikers will be awed by the vertical orientation of the metamorphic rocks along this section of trail. Our arrival at lovely Shadow Lake is via a notch in the metamorphic rocks, where we have a water-level view of the lake, with the grand Ritter Range as a backdrop. Camping is wisely restricted at this heavily overused lake, and only a few fair campsites may be found. We strongly discourage camping here, to help the lake in its recovery.

Southwest from Shadow Lake the trail ascends near rushing Shadow Creek. Several cascades along the stream invite the traveler to stop and rest, and there are deep holes for fishing or for swimming (in late season). For a mile above the inlet to Shadow Lake we are on the John Muir Trail; then it branches off north toward Thousand Island Lake. Our route continues upstream near Shadow Creek for about 1½ miles to Ediza Lake, where camping is allowed only on the north shore.

From here one can retrace one's steps to Agnew Meadows via Shadow Creek, but the experienced backpacker can make an interesting loop, or a shuttle via Devils Postpile. A faint, unmaintained trail switchbacks south from the southeast end of Ediza Lake up a steep, willow-covered slope. Parts of the trail are overgrown and it crosses several runoff streamlets, but it is easily followed as far as Iceberg Lake.

At the top of the first rise, we see below us the glacial cirque that holds Ediza Lake, and to the northwest, through a notch, there is a memorable view of Banner and Ritter. On the east, the massive heights of Volcanic Ridge dominate the horizon. We ascend through several little meadows covered with lupine and heather, and finally reach Iceberg Lake. From the outlet the footpath around the east side of the lake occasionally becomes lost in the talus as we ascend to the outlet of Cecile Lake. This stretch often has icy snow on it in early to mid season, and inexperienced backpackers *should not attempt it.*

Cecile Lake has the choicest views of the Minarets, and one will certainly want a camera there. Our obscure, partly ducked route skirts the lake on its east side to the southeast end of the lake, from which we have awesome views of Clyde Minaret, Minaret Lake and Minaret Creek canyon. From here, one can

Ediza Lake   *Jeff Schaffer*

either head back or drop down 500 feet to Minaret Lake, on
the vague trail to the east.

A long loop return may be made from Minaret Lake to
Agnew Meadows, or one may shuttle from Devils Postpile or
hitch-hike out from there. The Minaret Lake trail (Backpack
Trail #4) leads out to Devils Postpile. To make the loop back
to Agnew Meadows, take the Minaret Lake trail as far as
Johnston Meadow and then head north on the Muir Trail to
Shadow Lake. From there the first 3 miles of the Ediza Lake
trail return one to Agnew Meadows. This would take a day
from Minaret Lake.

BACKPACK TRAIL #8

Thousand Island Lake via the River Trail (7½ mi.)

The River Trail, which parallels the upper Middle Fork of
the San Joaquin River to its source, Thousand Island Lake, is
the least scenic route to the lake. However, an interesting and
dramatic return from the lake can be made via the High Trail
(Backpack Trail #9).

Our signed route leaves the south side of the second
parking lot just past Agnew Meadows Pack Station (map section D2) and follows the beginning of the Ediza Lake trail
(Backpack Trail #7) to a fork just beyond Olaine Lake. Here
we take the right (N) fork and climb steeply up from the river
for a while, until the trail's ascent becomes gentler under
fairly dense lodgepole pines. The sound of the cascading San
Joaquin River is a pleasant accompaniment to this dusty
climb up the canyon, and several nice campsites can be found
among junipers and aspens along this stretch of trail. We
cross several streamlets coming down from the Sierra crest
on the east before arriving at the Agnew Pass trail, which
climbs steeply through open lodgepole pine and sagebrush to
the High Trail, and then goes on to Agnew Pass.

The River Trail continues up the canyon, passes the steep Garnet Lake lateral, and slants upward away from the river to join the Pacific Crest Trail and High Trail coming in from the right (E). At this junction the River Trail officially ends, and we continue west on the High Trail (Backpack Trail #9) to Thousand Island Lake.

BACKPACK TRAIL #9

Thousand Island Lake via the High Trail (8 mi.)

This alternative to taking the River Trail (Backpack Trail #8) to Thousand Island Lake affords panoramic views of the Minarets, Mr. Ritter and Banner Peak, as well as glimpses down into the deep, glaciated canyon of the Middle Fork San Joaquin River. The High Trail can be combined with the River Trail to form an exciting loop trip between Agnew Meadows and Thousand Island Lake. This trail is now part of the Canada-to-Mexico Pacific Crest Trail.

The High Trail begins at the first parking lot north of Agnew Meadows Pack Station (map section D2). This trail starts with several long switchbacks in red-fir forest which take us up behind the pack station. Then we emerge from timber into open sagebrush scrub and, climbing steadily along the east wall of the Middle Fork canyon, we come to a vista point opposite the U-shaped canyon of Shadow Creek just before 1½ miles of trailside springs. This view is one of the most impressive sites along the route. The gouging power of glaciers during the Ice Age is attested to by the deeply scarred Middle Fork canyon and the hanging valley of Shadow Creek— formed by a tributary glacier—dropping steeply to the main valley below.

From this point the trail undulates along, trending upward, through a ground cover of mostly sagebrush, bitterbrush, willow and some mountain alders. Each time the trail descends

to one of the many tributaries of the San Joaquin River, the traveler will observe a lush growth of wildflowers, including larkspur, lupine, shooting star, columbine, penstemon, monkey flower, scarlet gilia and tiger lily.

Just before the High Trail begins its descent to meadowy Badger Lakes, a signed cut-off to Agnew Pass and Clark Lakes (Lateral Trail #3) forks to the right (north). We continue toward Badger Lakes, crossing the Agnew Pass trail, which connects Agnew Pass to the right with the River Trail to the left (south) via a steep path. Just beyond marshy Badger Lakes, the trail to Agnew Pass and Clark Lakes rejoins our route. Continuing on the High Trail, we roll gently through open lodgepole pine, and then switchback down to a junction with the River Trail on the slopes above the upper reaches of the Middle Fork. At this junction we turn right and climb around a knob that separates our route from the river. For the next ½ mile we pass above several meadows and tarns on a recently rerouted section of trail to arrive at the outlet of Thousand Island Lake and another trail junction, this time with the John Muir Trail. Our trek ends here at the lake, where campsites with awe-inspiring views up-lake of Banner Peak, Mt. Ritter and Glacier Pass can be had along both the north and south shores—though the south shore tends to be less populated. Camping is *not* allowed within ¼ mile of the outlet.

BACKPACK TRAIL #10

Lake George to Deer Lakes (5½ mi.)

The Deer Lakes trail along Mammoth Crest essentially deadends in a glaciated basin, the former route down Deer Creek from the lakes having been abandoned. This trail offers vistas of much of *Devils Postpile* quadrangle, rivaling those from Mammoth Mountain itself.

Left: Shadow Lake and the Ritter Range

First we follow the Crystal Lake trail (Day Hike #2) until it branches left (south), then continue climbing in pumice and granite gravel (also known as grus) to the right (SW). We soon surmount a ridge and see a panorama extending from Banner Peak and Mt. Ritter in the west to Mammoth Mountain in the north and Gold Mountain and Coldwater Canyon in the east. From this viewpoint, switchbacks take us up toward Mammoth Crest through lodgepole pine, western white pine and mountain hemlock into a thinning stand of whitebark pine. Where the scattered trees have been flattened into *krummholz* form by wind and snow, granite-and-pumice footing gives way to reddish cinders, remnants of an Ice-Age cinder cone.

Though the John Muir Wilderness Boundary is actually on the crest ahead, we pass a sign for it on our ascent here. This 500,000-acre preserve—California's largest—is named for the famed naturalist. First set aside in 1931 (as the High Sierra Primitive Area) by authority of the Secretary of Agriculture, it extends from here southward along the Sierra crest to peaks south of Mt. Whitney. At a trail fork beyond this sign, we go right, upward toward the cindery ridge to the west. The left (south) fork, which crosses what seems to be the remnant of the cinder cone's crater, can be taken on our return trip. Climbing upward again, we pass a faint, abandoned trail which drops steeply north toward Mammoth Pass. We finally gain the crest, and much of the area of *Devils Postpile* quadrangle is visible from the summit of this cone. We can make out both the Middle Fork and the North Fork of the San Joaquin, the Ritter Range, Mammoth Mountain, and of course the Mammoth Crest.

Proceeding southward along the crest, we intersect in less than ½ mile the "hypoteneuse" trail across the cinder cone's remnant crater that we bypassed at the last fork. We can take this shortcut on our return from Deer Lakes. Our route ahead crosses an arid-looking saddle with scattered whitebark pines separated by large expanses of cindery, granity gravel.

Judging by the sparseness of vegetation and the exposure to winds here, one may reasonably conclude that the precipitation actually available to plants on this ridge might be no more than that which commonly defines a desert: 10 inches or less annually. Since high winds accompany most of the winter snowstorms that supply the bulk of this region's moisture, and since winds are most intense on summits like this, only a few inches of snow may accumulate here, compared to the hundreds that build up on both sides of the crest. So this saddle can possibly be considered arid, even though it is in a region of moderate precipitation.

As our route gets rocky and begins a steep ascent up the west side of the ridge through a stand of whitebark pine, Fish Valley comes into sight below to the southwest. The path tops the ridge at 11,200 feet at a gap called a *col,* and we can now see all the way to the White Mountains on the Nevada border to the east. In between lie Coldwater Canyon, Gold Mountain and Glass Mountain ridge. (Here the trail goes off *Devils Postpile* quad to the east and enters *Mt. Morrison.*) From this col we round a shoulder and drop steeply down through whitebark pines to the outlet of the northernmost of the three Deer Lakes. Sheltered campsites are on the west and south sides, and an inviting little beach beckons at the northwest corner of the lake.

Faint trails lead from this lake through meadows and dense but scrubby whitebark pine to the upper lake, where camping is most sheltered around the outlet. The cirque that these lakes lie in offers opportunities for leisurely wandering over talus slopes, moraines, and wet meadows thick with red and white heather, dwarf willow and Labrador tea. The lowest of the three lakes is the most heavily used, and it has the poorest campsites.

BACKPACK TRAIL #11

Granite Creek Campground to Twin Island Lakes
(15½ mi.)

This trail begins at a trailhead in the *Merced Peak* quadrangle, with road access from the west side of the Sierra, and leads to dramatic and remote camping on the little-visited west side of the Ritter Range. It begins, as the Isberg Trail, northeast of Granite Creek Campground along Forest Road 4S57 (west of map section A5). Due to current (1989) logging operations in the area, the trailhead is poorly marked, and may be difficult to locate. Look for it while heading east on the new road around Granite Creek Campground ¼ mile past its intersection with the old road leaving the northeast corner of the campground. There is parking on the south side of the road just beyond the trailhead.

Our route proceeds up the drainage of East Fork Granite Creek, an area closed to motor vehicles. The forest cover here consists mostly of large Jeffrey and lodgepole pines, with young white and red firs in the understory. When fires are absent, the shade-tolerant firs normally supplant the pines in forest succession. Otherwise, the fire-tolerant pines remain dominant.

After a moderate climb of about 2 miles, the trail comes out onto a brush-covered slope above East Fork Granite Creek and traverses through manzanita, huckleberry oak and gooseberry to Granite Creek Niche, where the East Fork rushes through a narrow gap—the "Niche"—between two granite shoulders. We enter Ansel Adams Wilderness here, but the boundary was unsigned in 1989. Camping is good at the Niche.

Leaving the Niche, we parallel the stream and soon arrive at a junction from which the Isberg trail continues north to Yosemite National Park. Our route—now the Stevenson trail—crosses East Fork Granite Creek and then passes through a meadow that is being overrun by young lodgepole pines but is still open enough to have a cover of cottony knotweed, yellow meadow monkey flowers, lavender shooting stars and large-leafed corn lilies. In ⅓ mile we pass the Cora Creek trail (Lateral Trail #1) and then begin a long stroll through lodgepole-pine forest. Only the tinkling note of the dark-eyed junco and the eerie fluting of the hermit thrush interrupt our solitude. A quarter mile into our stroll we pass the Chetwood Trail going off to the left at an obscure and poorly marked fork. We turn right here and then ford Cora Creek shortly beyond. There are few hikers on this trail.

One mile past Cora Creek, as we approach Chetwood Creek, we enter *Devils Postpile* quadrangle. Following blazes through lodgepole pine and red fir, we finally break out into open aspen and sagebrush. Our route then switchbacks up a dry slope, and we soon come to "Surprise Saddle." Here a fine vista of the west side of the Ritter Range sloping down into the North Fork of the San Joaquin river greets the eye. The classic U-shaped, glaciated canyons of Dike and Iron creeks, the knife-edged ridge of the Minarets, and extensive glacial polish offer a dramatic, first-hand view of the effects of glaciation. Off in the south, the confluence of the three forks of the San Joaquin River is evident, and down in the canyon below we can make out a gaging-station cabin on the North Fork. This wild country was finally accorded statutory protection in 1984 when it was incorporated into Ansel Adams Wilderness Area.

Entering a mixed forest of red fir, mountain hemlock and silver pine, dotted with large fields of blue lupine, we begin a long descent to Hemlock Crossing. Our path leaves the *Devils Postpile* map briefly here and then re-enters it as we cross a small stream and start to drop in earnest toward the North Fork. The trail soon becomes extremely steep and rocky. Firs and hemlocks on this steep slope are permanently warped at their bases, due to the deep winter snows that bent them to the ground as seedlings and saplings.

Hemlock Crossing on the North Fork

At the end of a 1300-foot descent, we arrive at Hemlock Crossing. Here the North Fork breaks through the beds of westward-dipping strata it has been paralleling, and plunges into a wide pool—ideal for swimming late in the season, when the water level is lower and the temperature is higher. This is an excellent place to camp. Strangely, there are no hemlocks right at Hemlock Crossing, but there are 3 or 4 downstream, below the campsite.

Our route as we leave Hemlock Crossing for Twin Island Lakes crosses the river at the bridge, passes the Iron Creek trail (Lateral Trail #2) going right (south), and climbs north up the east side of Slide Creek past many blossoms of penstemon, lupine, azalea and paintbrush. Below us water ouzels bob up and down on rocks in the creek.

The trail several times ascends and levels off over a series of benches as we climb up the east canyon wall. This steplike relief is largely due to underlying beds of rock, which have differential resistance to erosion. The topography is in turn reponsible for the collection of rain and snowmelt water into the ponds we see in various stages of ecological succession—

from open water to meadow to forest—for the next 2 miles along the trail. Mosquitoes, as a consequence, are dense all along the route from early to mid season. Stands of lodgepole pine, Jeffrey pine and red fir are interspersed with brushy patches of sagebrush, huckleberry oak and pinemat manzanita. Then we pass through dusty "Lonesome Joe Camp" and climb to the easy crossing of Slide Creek.

Here we enter what is shown on the map as one big "Stevenson Meadow," but is actually a series of wet meadows separated by stands of trees. The wildflower show compares with any in the Sierra: shooting star, monkey flower, penstemon, corn lily, larkspur, knotweed, groundsel, forget-me-not and mountain aster are especially evident in mid season. Unfortunately, the peak of blooming seems to coincide with the peak of mosquitoes, and insect repellent is essential at this time of year. As the trail leaves Stevenson Meadow and climbs west above the cascading North Fork, we have better views ahead of the ridge on the southeast boundary of Yosemite National Park, topped by Electra and Rodgers peaks.

Just past the roaring junction with Bench Canyon, the North Fork veers northeast, and there is excellent camping here in a heavy growth of lodgepole, fir and hemlock. From this point on to Twin Island Lakes, the trail becomes increasingly difficult to follow, and only experienced hikers should continue. The route is often over glacially polished rock, and there are only occasional ducks to mark the path. Where there is vegetation, the trail is poorly blazed and often overgrown with willows and shrubs. However, the rewards in solitude and scenic beauty which lie ahead are well worth the effort.

Our route climbs away from the river before traversing back toward it, at a higher elevation. Then we drop slightly into a meadow, the North Fork flowing rather placidly on our left. For the next 2 miles the trail alternately leads away from the

North Fork across meadows and snowmelt streams and climbs back toward the river on glacially polished metavolcanic rocks. Occasional stands of red fir and lodgepole pine offer sheltered and definitely uncrowded camping. Where there are trees along the trail, the blazes are usually either grown over or nonexistent, so we have to rely on ducks to find the route.

As the trail approaches the stream draining Ritter Lakes and Lake Catherine, it veers east away from the North Fork into a long sagebrush-and-grass meadow. When the falls of the stream finally come into sight, the hiker can make a difficult ford easier by crossing near the river or close to the falls. Once past this obstacle, the experienced hiker should be able to pick out the ducked route to Glacier Pass and to follow it up to the base of the cliffs, where it strikes eastward. The route to Twin Island Lakes leaves cross country from this point, heading almost due west and somewhat upward through the gap that lies just east of the more northern and larger of the Twin Island Lakes. Camping at the larger lake is best either near the inlet on the north end or on a point of the eastern shore opposite the islands.

Not many travelers get to Twin Island Lakes or to the lakes higher up the North Fork watershed. Solitude reigns. Among the few sounds striking the alpine listener's ears are the raucous calls of the ubiquitous Clark's nutcracker, the squeaking of a cony and the rustling of breezes through stunted whitebark pine. Cinquefoil, penstemon, mountain aster and red heather highlight the glacially eroded landscape with spots of color. The water is clear and cold, and the alpenglow on Mt. Davis and other, unnamed peaks to the north is rarely excelled. The way to Twin Island Lakes is difficult, but the rewards are great.

LATERAL TRAIL #1

Cora Creek Trail to the North Fork
San Joaquin River (4½ mi.)

This lateral leads to good fishing and secluded camping on the San Joaquin River's North Fork. It leaves the Twin Island Lakes Trail (Backpack Trail #11) about ½ mile north of the Niche, which lies just off the *Devils Postpile* quadrangle in *Merced Peak* (west of map section A4). This dusty path starts southeast through a stand of red fir and lodgepole pine, and then quickly veers east at a junction with the Green Mountain stock driveway from Soldier Meadow. Dropping east, the trail soon reaches the south bank of Cora Creek (dry in late season). As the descent becomes steeper, the North Fork canyon and the west side of the Ritter Range near Iron Mountain come into sight. One cannot help noticing the contrast in vegetation between the cool, moist, north-facing slope we are walking down and the dry, south-facing slope across Cora Creek. Whereas this shadier side has a dense cover of white fir, willow and dwarf maple, the opposite side is mostly covered with brush, such as huckleberry oak and manzanita.

We continue to drop over several steplike benches down to the North Fork San Joaquin. Fording the river is easy here only in late season, when snowmelt runoff is at a minimum; one must be cautious when crossing earlier in the year. Beyond the ford our route starts up the east side of the North Fork, where conditions are somewhat drier, and the dominant plants are drought-resistant huckleberry oak, manzanita, and juniper with occasional Jeffrey pines.

After ½ mile the trail turns to leave the river. Ahead lies a good campsite, but our path makes a short, steep ascent, up what becomes a cascading streamlet in early season, to a bench where knee-deep Lily Lake lies behind a *roche moutonee* (see the chapter "Geology") above the river. This lake is undergoing succession from pond to forest, as litter and silt over the centuries have been filling it in and terrestrial plants have encroached from the surrounding forest. In late season red-brown bracken ferns, golden aspens and yellow willows give Lily Lake a welcome tint of fall color. Beyond Lily Lake we climb slightly and then descend to a good, well-developed campsite on a bench just above some river pools. About ¼ mile beyond this campsite is the North Fork gaging-station cabin. Water data gathered here are used to predict spring and summer runoff in the San Joaquin Valley.

Beyond the cabin, the trail quickly ends, though a ducked route continues up-river along brushy, rocky slopes and benches. One can continue on this route to the mouth of Iron Creek, climbing up and over rocky benches where necessary. From Iron Creek diagonal climbing northeast up brushy slopes leads to the 77 Corral/Hemlock Crossing Trail (Lateral Trail #2).

Lateral Trail #2
77 Corral to Hemlock Crossing (7 mi.)

This lateral runs from the Devils Postpile/Granite Creek Trail at 77 Corral north to the Granite Creek/Twin Island Lakes trail at Hemlock Crossing on North Fork San Joaquin River. It gives access from the Devils Postpile area to the remote headwaters of the San Joaquin west of the Ritter Range, near the southeastern edge of Yosemite National Park.

From 77 Corral (map section B4) we proceed northwest toward Iron Creek. Indeed, our route is known as the Iron Creek trail, and it is well-maintained though marked by many unnecessary ducks. At first we climb almost imperceptibly through open forest to a fair campsite on Cargyle Creek. Continuing upward more steeply onto a dry, west-facing slope, we begin to encounter scattered sagebrush among the trees. Then we break out into Headquaters Meadow, where sagebrush is being invaded by lodgepole pine and even red fir. Because the vegetation is short, we have a fine vista from here to the south, where the canyons of the North and Middle forks of the San Joaquin River join below Junction Bluffs.

Our path passes through a stand of red fir and then emerges into Earthquake Meadow, where numerous signs mark a trail junction. A 2-mile lateral leads southwest to Snake Meadow, and our route continues northwest toward Iron Creek. Leaving Earthquake Meadow, we descend gently through open white-fir forest with a huckleberry and bush-chinquapin understory. After a level segment, the trail begins ascending across a large meadow that slopes away in the west toward the North Fork San Joaquin. Here one may ponder the picturesque, snow-bent aspens, which are especially beautiful in fall after their leaves have turned golden yellow. They have a fragile beauty that is singularly welcome among the faded browns of autumn.

Beyond this unnamed meadow our well-blazed trail rolls along for a mile in a varied forest and then drops sharply down to Iron Creek. Where it levels off about a hundred yards below the creek crossing, there is good camping in a stand of Jeffrey pine, white fir, Sierra juniper and lodgepole pine. We continue on our trail and switchback down steeply across a dry, southwest-facing slope covered with a dense growth of huckleberry oak, sagebrush and manzanita. Then we cross a loose talus slope of sharp metamorphic rocks, which could be slippery, particularly when wet or icy. After this quick drop, we pass near the North Fork and begin the riverside stretch of our route. First we ascend very gently about ¾ mile through a series of wet meadows inhabited by willows, tall grass and water-tolerant species such as red dogwood and aspen, to Dike Creek. Here there is a packer campsite just below a beautiful cascade that feeds a pool on the river.

A short, rocky climb from Dike Creek takes us onto a rocky ridge, which blocks the river from our view, but up and down the valley we can see the typical U-shaped cross section of a glaciated canyon. Our climb quickly eases off, and on leveller footing we approach another beautiful cascade splashing into a tempting pool. In another minute we reach a junction at yet a third cascade and pool. The trail to Granite Creek immediately crosses the North Fork on a sturdy steel bridge, and a huge campsite is found on the opposite side. Hemlock Crossing is an excellent place to camp, and from here the Twin Island Lakes trail can be taken to the remote headwaters of the North Fork, which has over a dozen lakes in a very alpine setting. Several lakes lie near the bases of Banner Peak and Mt. Ritter. Camping among these remote lakes offers far more wilderness solitude than at the lakes east of the summits.

LATERAL TRAIL #3

High Trail to Agnew Pass, Clark Lakes and Badger Lakes (2 mi.)

This lateral from the High Trail (Backpack Trail #9) takes us over the Sierra crest at Agnew Pass into the drainage of Rush Creek at Clark Lakes, and then returns to the High Trail just west of Badger Lakes.

About one mile southeast of Badger Lakes, the High Trail from Agnew Meadows begins a gentle descent. Here (map section C1) our signed lateral to Agnew Pass and Clark Lakes forks to the right (NW). On it we traverse a slope covered with sagebrush and a few scattered lodgepole pines. Purplish mountain aster, scarlet gilia and yellowish mule ears are seen on this slope from mid to late season. Our route soon intersects the Agnew Pass trail, and we turn right (north) onto it. About 400 yards up this trail we cross Agnew Pass at Summit Lake, where camping is good from early to mid season.

Beyond Agnew Pass our trail circles the largest of the Clark Lakes, and we pass two trails near its outlet. (The first goes northeast past the highest of the Clark Lakes in lovely meadows full of wild onions and then drops through Spooky Meadows and eventually goes to Agnew and Silver lakes. The second trail—which we meet across the outlet stream—heads downhill 2 miles in lodgepole pine and meets the Rush Creek trail at Lower Rush Meadow, just off the quadrangle.) Camping is good east and west of this lake near the open meadowy areas, and rainbow trout are numerous.

Our trail continues around the west side of this lake and then climbs through open whitebark pine and mountain hemlock past several other lakes of the Clark Lakes group, which may be dry in late season. Beyond the last of the Clark Lakes, we glimpse Thousand Island Lake and Banner Peak in the west before dropping through open lodgepole, sagebrush and snowberry toward Badger Lakes, visible below. Our route rejoins the High Trail about ¼ mile west of Badger Lakes.

Largest of the Clark Lakes

LATERAL TRAIL #4

Lower Marie Lake (1½ mi.)

Lower and Upper Marie Lakes are high-elevation glacial lakes which offer exhilarating and secluded camping close to the heavily travelled John Muir Trail.

The trail to Marie Lakes takes off (map section A1) from the Muir Trail northbound (Backpack Trail #1) about ¾ mile northwest of Rush Creek. It switchbacks gently upward on granite and then levels off some through meadows with scattered patches of willows and whitebark pines. Fine campsites with excellent views present themselves near the Marie Lakes outlet stream below.

Our well-graded route soon resumes its switchbacking ascent, now up the south wall of the canyon, where lupine plus alpine sorrel and other high-elevation flowers can be seen from mid to late season. In early season here the trail is likely to be covered with late-lingering snow, but you should be able to see ducks marking the route.

Lower Marie Lake

We next surmount a ridge with superb views of the Ritter
and Cathedral ranges close at hand in the west, as well as the
more distant peaks of the Sierra crest in the east. After a short
descent, we are near the northeast corner of Lower Marie Lake
where scattered camps can be made in the rocks near the
outlet. Camping here is exposed and windy but highly scenic,
with Mt. Lyell and Rodgers Peak looming above to the west. A
short cross-country jaunt along the west side of the lake takes
one to Upper Marie Lake, one mile away.

LATERAL TRAIL #5
Iron Lake Trail (4 mi.)

Due to limited camping space at Iron Lake's neighbor and
none at the lake itself, you may want to make this route a day
excursion from the Corral Meadow area.

The trail starts at 77 Corral (map section B4) going north
along a fenced-in grazing area, then leaves the shade of
lodgepoles for that of red firs and western white pines as it
switchbacks up to the crest of a large glacial moraine. You stay
on the crest momentarily, then contour over to a seasonal
creeklet draining a typical Sierran meadow rich in corn lilies.
About ½ mile beyond it and 2 miles from the trail's start, you
reach a usually flowing creek. From it you can start a ducked
cross-country route that traverses a bit over ½ mile west to
shallow Strobe Lake. The Iron Lake trail, however, climbs
another ¼ mile to smaller, shallower Alstot Lake. There's a
good, though somewhat small, campsite beneath lodgepoles by
the lake, and we recommend you backpack no farther than this
site.

From Alstot Lake's south shore the trail now starts an
almost continuously steep ascent to a windy saddle, reaching it
and its alpine flora in just under one mile and about 1000 feet

above the lake. Take plenty of rest stops to admire the southern views you get on your way up. From the saddle you have another set of views, these of course dominated by the Ritter Range. Some mountaineers prefer to reach Iron Lake by hiking cross-country east up Iron Creek, leaving Lateral Trail #2 about 1¾ miles south-southeast of Hemlock Crossing. Should you take this route, end the cross-country part of it by climbing to the alpine saddle that the Iron Lake trail crosses. In most years there is a sizable snowfield extending north down from the saddle.

On a tread blasted in bedrock, you curve east from the saddle and traverse ¼ mile to a chilly, somewhat shallow lakelet. This is the real "iron lake," since a deposit of iron lies

Iron Lake   *Jeff Schaffer*

in the metavolcanic rocks just above its southwest shore. A perennial snowfield usually hides most of the deposit from view.

At the lakelet you'll find a one-person and a two-person campsite, both receiving token protection from the winds by scrubby whitebark pines. The trail ends here, but you can easily reach the named lake by heading across a talus slope to an obvious notch above the far side of the lakelet. From the notch, barren Iron Lake lies just below you, confined by bedrock walls and talus slopes. No campsites exist. Iron Mountain, looming ominously above the lake, presents a technically easy ascent—little more than a walk-up. However, lots of loose rock exists, so be careful and take your time.

LATERAL TRAIL #6
San Joaquin River Forks Trail (2½ mi.)

This lateral drops about 1500 feet to the lowest campsite described in this book. The trail, which is quite easy to follow even though it is only irregularly maintained, is very steep, very bouldery and, and on a sunny afternoon, very hot. Rattlesnakes may be encountered along the trail or around the super campsite at trail's end.

The trail starts ¾ mile southeast of Sheep Crossing, as it leaves Backpack Trail #3 and curves south along a series of broad, granitic benches. After ⅔ mile you reach an excellent viewpoint and see "pyramidal" Junction Butte, directly across the canyon. This somewhat forested landmark has been strongly abraded by glaciers on all sides. To its right, about 5¾ miles from your viewpoint, Balloon Dome, with steep slopes of naked granodiorite, pierces the skyline. Like its more famous look-alike, Yosemite's Mt. Starr King, it achieved its domelike form millions of years before it was ever glaciated, and it does not owe its shape to the work of glaciers, though they certainly smoothed its sides to some extent.

To the left of Junction Butte you see a large, dark remnant of an andesite lava flow that is roughly 3½ million years old. Another remnant, which you may have already noticed, lies immediately above the granitic benches you've just traversed.

Seasoned Sierra hikers know that streams flowing across glaciated granitic landscapes can become quite dry in mid or late season, and therefore the steep descent you are about to make down south-facing granitic slopes could be intolerably hot and dry. However, thanks to the water-retaining volcanic rocks just above you, a spring-fed creeklet flows down the hot slopes all summer long. About ½ mile east of your viewpoint you reach this creeklet and then descend very steeply alongside it, finally crossing it after a drop of about 400 feet. On a merely steep grade you descend ⅔ mile before you come within about 200 feet of the pools, rapids and cascades of the "chorusing" North Fork San Joaquin River. Over the remaining ½ mile you have access to many pools and could make camp on any of a number of nearby benches. The large flat near the trail's end, covered with an open spread of Jeffrey pines and incense-cedars, offers more camping possibilities. However, at trail's end lies a moderately large campsite beneath tall alders, maples and live oaks. One or more persons went through great effort to make it a home away from home, and it is equipped with tables, benches, storage shelves and a well-built rock-and-mortar stove. Camped near the union of the boisterous North and Middle forks, opposite a massive granitic monolith, one could happily stay here for days, enjoying the scenery and the ambience of this Junction Butte country. If you hanker to swim in the area's many pools, plan for a mid or late August trip, when the water warms up to the low or mid 60s and the current has slackened enough for safe swimming.

RECOMMENDED READING

Farquhar, Francis P., *History of the Sierra Nevada.* Berkeley: U.C. Press. 1969

Hill, Mary, *Geology of the Sierra Nevada.* Berkeley: U.C. Press, 1975

Huber, N. K., and C. D. Rinehart. *Cenozoic Volcanic Rocks of the Devils Postpile Quadrangle, Eastern Sierra Nevada, California* (Map GQ-437). U.S. Geological Survey, 1967

Huber, N. K., and Wymond Eckhardt, *Devils Postpile Story.* Three Rivers, California: Sequoia Natural History Association, 1985

McMinn, Howard E. and Evelyn Maino, *Pacific Coast Trees.* Berkeley: U.C. Press, 1959

Munz, Philip A., *California Mountain Wildflowers.* Berkeley: U.C. Press, 1968

Peters, Ed, *Mountaineering, the Freedom of the Hills.* Seattle: The Mountaineers, 1982

Peterson, P. Victor and P. Victor, Jr., *Native Trees of the Sierra Nevada.* Berkeley: U.C. Press, 1975

Rinehart, C. D., et al., *Mammoth Lakes Sierra.* Mammoth Lakes: Genny Smith Books, 1989

Robbins, Chandler, S., et al., *Birds of North America.* New York: Golden. 1983

Roper, Steve, *Climbers Guide to the High Sierra.* San Francisco: Sierra Club, 1976

Scott, Shirley, L., ed., *Field Guide to the Birds of North America.* National Geographic Society, 1983

Starr, Walter A. Jr., *Starr's Guide to the John Muir Trail.* San Francisco: Sierra Club, 1974

Storer, Tracy I. and Robert L. Usinger, *Sierra Nevada Natural History,* Berkeley: U.C. Press, 1963

Whitney, Stephen, *The Sierra Nevada, A Sierra Club Naturalist's Guide.* San Francisco: Sierra Club, 1979

Other relevant Wilderness Press publications

Guide to the John Muir Trail (2nd edition, 1984)

Pacific Crest Trail, v. 1, California (4th edition, 1989)

Place Names of the Sierra Nevada (1st edition, 1986)

Sierra Nevada Flora (3rd edition, 1986)

Sierra North (5th edition, 1985)

Tuolumne Meadows High Sierra Hiking Guide #4 (2nd edition, 1977)

Yosemite National Park (2nd edition, 1983)

Index

Acknowledgments

This guidebook in all its editions, could not have been written without the kind assistance of many mountain friends. I'd like to thank especially for all their help and patience Van Collingsworth, Lina Martin, Bob Grom, Larry Eastman and Mark Clark of the Mammoth Ranger District, Inyo National Forest; Gary Ogden, Wymond Eckhardt, Jim Magill and Leslie Brandlin of the National Park Service at Devils Postpile; Bill Skovran of Sierra National Forest; and Jeff Schaffer and Tom Winnett of Wilderness Press.

       — Ron Felzer
       Kensington, California
       January 1990